"*Easily You* is a hug for the soul. So many business books tell you what to do and how to build your professional life, but no one takes the time to analyse and relate to how we feel while we embark on our intense professional journey. *Easily You* is a poetic and insightful read for anyone who feels overwhelmed and out of focus in their life."

Ana Paula Tediosi, Ambitious Working Mother of two,
Author of "Ambition Factor: Rewrite the story of working mothers"

"A naked portrayal, a call to who we already are. Elodie eloquently weaves poetry, wonderings and simple stories that speaks to us all – whether entrepreneur, scientist, artist or politician. In times of plentiful distractions to choose from, she reminds us that our wellbeing is present and speaking right now, through us."

Dana Klepper-Smith, Body and Soul Researcher,
Founder of Breath for Business

"Elodie's life stories – embracing meticulous prose and impalpable poem – are touching, honest and surprising. She documents her journey with talent and courage, inspiring us all to take authentic ownership of our lives."

Lorenzo Garofano, Co-Founder, Head of Sales
and Marketing at Xilva AG

"We have been connecting with stories since we were children. Elodie's story is no different. A strong, yet sensible woman in search of constant transformation. It is an important reminder for us to be. Not to be like her, but just to be ourselves."

Kalina Juzwiak, Multimedia Artist and Mentor,
helping artists live from their art

"Elodie Caucigh has written a wonderfully honest and important book about letting go of our self-deceptive stories. *Easily You* reveals the dark side of the glamorous startup world and the illusions of pursuing false dreams, and shows how to break free from the vicious circle we got ourselves into with the help of our wellbeing."

Felix Hofmann, Independent Scientist
studying the psychology of innovation

"This book is an unvarnished and reflective recording of a real and pressing issue in the new reality. As a self-efficacy advocate, I can recommend it to anyone who wants to break out of the pre-set norms, discover and live out their true self."

Patrycja Pielaszek, Playful Business Transformator.
Passionate Culture & Community Builder

"Elodie's book is unlike any book I've read in the space of wellbeing. Published at an opportune time, her readers will gain valuable nuggets of insights without being preached to. It's like being right there with her and having the privilege to be a witness to her story in all its pain, vulnerability, courage and finally, her return to herself."

Karina Schneider, Mother, Personal Leadership Coach,
Mental Health First Aid Instructor

"*Easily You* is more a poem than a book. An activation of prose to make you comfortable in the uncomfortable. My advice is to open *Easily You* to a random page – absorb and react."

Michelle Gasparovic, Entrepreneur, Designer

"*Easily You* is truly different. Deep, beautifully written, and thought-provoking. A celebration of our wellbeing: of the good stuff but also of its suffocating pains and calls for attention. *Easily You* is one of these books that leaves a mark – and yet that you absolutely need to keep in close reach in case you ever need a tonic and fresh reminder that all you really need to do is be you! "

Marie Stoecklin, Faculty Developer,
Learning Design Specialist and Psychologist

"Elodie's book is both poetic and wise. Simply reading it is wellbeing and relaxing in itself!"

Lisa Falco, PhD, AI consultant, Mother of two,
Author of "Go Figure! The astonishing science of the female body"

"While reading, it feels like your mind is talking to you – a raw expression of sentiments that question your being, in a challenging but somehow comforting way. Someone else is sharing those doubts, those feelings: Elodie has put them into words."

Maja Juzwiak, Photographer and Storyteller living in hotels

"A must read for anyone who thought, like me, that wellbeing was something we must check off at the end of our day, something we must do, rather than something we already have and are, easily."

Assem Klammsteiner, Founder and Owner of Simply Soup,
Self-development Junkie

"What an honest, thought-provoking, touching and fun read! Elodie is a true artist. Joining her on her journey of finding what feels good, discovering lots of ways that don't work and some that do, you'll see wellbeing in a whole new light. If you're looking for more fulfilment, success and peace of mind, this book is a treasure trove."

Melanie Kovacs, Founder of Joypreneurs

"Absolutely gorgeous. Poetic. Relatable. Elodie shares her depths so eloquently and helps open us to our own."

Elise Dorsett, Transformational Life Coach
and Mastermind Facilitator

Also by Elodie Caucigh:

re-set wellbeing cards, Exercise cards for wellbeing at the desk, real ease and Bright Lines Design, 2020

real ease on board, Inflight-yoga video series, real ease, 2019

easily you

Elodie Caucigh

easily you

WHEN WELLBEING WORKS FOR YOU

CLINK STREET PUBLISHING, LONDON

Published by Clink Street Publishing 2022

Cover Illustration: Kalina Juzwiak
Book cover and design: Francesca Poggi, Bright Lines Design
Content editing: Elodie Caucigh

First edition.

This book is for inspiration, information or educational purposes only and is not intended to act as a substitute for medical advice or treatment. Any person with a condition requiring medical attention should seek relevant support and consult a qualified medical practitioner, counsellor or suitable therapist.

ISBN: paperback

ISBN: ebook

for the whole of us

66 *Our deepest fear is not that we are inadequate.*
Our deepest fear is that we are powerful beyond measure.
It is our light, not our darkness, that most frightens us.
We ask ourselves, 'Who am I to be brilliant, gorgeous,
talented, fabulous?' Actually, who are you not to be? ...
Your playing small does not serve the world. There is nothing
enlightened about shrinking so that other people won't feel
insecure around you ... And as we let our own light shine,
we unconsciously give other people permission to do the
same. As we are liberated from our own fear, our presence
automatically liberates others.

Poem by Marianne Williamson[1]

Foreword

Stories – we all have them; we all are them. The stories we tell ourselves and the ones described by other people and circumstances. They can break us or make us, depending on where we stand: in line or out of line with ourselves.

Elodie's book shows us the wild variety of situations from her life that all of us – busy entrepreneurs, travellers of time, partners – can easily relate to. Life can get messy with the enormous abundance of ideas, possibilities, and ways of living or running a business. And life will tell us each time when we are not aligned with ourselves, when we (desperately) try to fit in places that are not meant for us.

And yet: yes, it is very much up to us what decisions we make. It lies in our hands to make decisions that are really ours and to ensure that whatever we do is aligned with who we are.

Sounds easy? But is it really? Diving into Elodie's world of wonder is a search for what matters most, an inspiration by raising questions and sharing observations. Maybe after this read, you will also ask yourself: *"When is wellbeing actually working for me?"* and start your journey of life leadership.

And then, perhaps just then – when we are cultivating it for ourselves – we can go out and inspire others and the world to do the same, to help make it a little better, one moment at the time.

As the wise words by environmentalist David W. Orr go: "the planet does not need more successful people. But it does desperately need more peacemakers, healers, restorers, storytellers, and lovers of every kind." I wish you, dear reader, to become one, perhaps simply by being more than doing, by finding your way to express your true self and ride on the wellbeing line that is yours.

Iwona Fluda,
Entrepreneur and Creativity Enthusiast

Self
without help

Why haven't I written an ultimate wellbeing guide on how to be fulfilled and productive, a better self with greater success and better health?

Isn't it what wellbeing and online marketing experts do these days? Isn't it what you, dear self-help reader and serial-improver are looking for, when you invest in yourself?

I know you put your time and money in this. So have I, and it didn't work for me.

So, I decided otherwise, voilà.

And I want to encourage *you* to decide otherwise. Re-voilà.

Your self – your unattended and frustrated genius, your unconventional animal, your censured artist and misunderstood visionary with a heart too big for this world to carry – needs more space to exist.

More than you dare to think.

You need space beyond the corners of yourself. You need freedom to let things bang against the walls.

I say this because it sounded good, elevating and so it took off, just like me.

On its own.

With an elan of justice to reclaim who you came here to be.

You.

But this time around, easily.

This is what wellbeing is all about.

Being easily you is about remembering how it feels to know. To know that *to be* is all you need *to do*. For the rest, your wellbeing is the one working for you. Not the other way round.

You may be too busy, too distracted by the noise and feeds, too broken by work and bills. But this can only change if you stop for a moment.

If you stop trying to cover yourself up. If you stop deceiving yourself under layers of excuses and never-ending to-dos. If you stop copying from borrowed agendas, moving fast in productivity quicksand and scaling up in lean business plans.

Stopping doesn't bring magic.
Stopping gives you the time and the space
to question. And as you start questioning
around you, you will start to feel and to
remember that you've known the answer.

Your answers are not mine to tell. But in this book, I can lend you some of the ones I found to reflect upon yourself.

In my questions and inspirations, in my aches and revelations, in my roars and rhymes as I surfed away from what wasn't mine and closer to myself.

OUT OF LINE
you will witness my strongest
rebellions and loudest calls for action.

ALONG THE LINE
you will read my self-consideration
and attempts for reconciliation.

IN LINE
you will stream smoothly with me,
at last with ease and certainty.

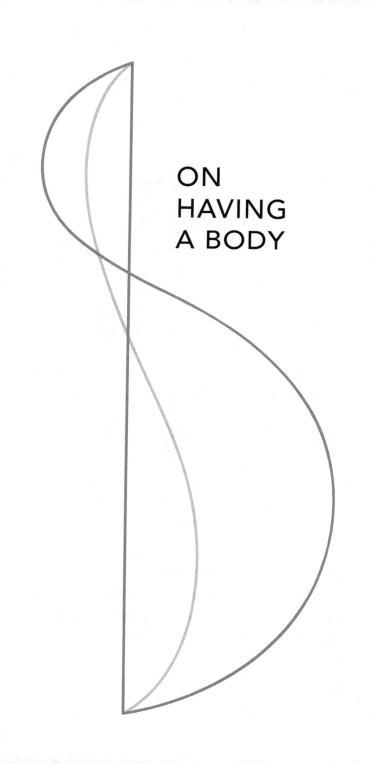

ON
HAVING
A BODY

Trespassing what is yuck

I sit at the doctor's practice in Strasbourg on a Wednesday. My father picked me up from the train station and came with me. I travelled from Zurich the same morning.

My stomach has been bothering me, I tell the doctor. *I feel nauseous after I eat, my belly swells up like a balloon and it is very uncomfortable. So, I sit at my desk like a zombie, slow and sluggish, waiting for it to pass. It also happens that I suddenly get cold sweat and panic because I am scared to vomit, so I run to the bathroom and breathe as slow and deep as I can. I usually manage to calm myself down. At night, I sit upright in my bed otherwise I feel sick to my stomach and have reflux. There too, my belly is so big that you would think I am pregnant.*

I don't know what's wrong, I don't know what to eat anymore... I think I have a milk allergy, could we do a test, please?

We won't do any allergy tests. No doctors in France agreed to do this. Neither the allergist, nor the gastroenterologist. The first one only asks me if I am stressed. I gasp, offended at her question, still I take a minute to think.

How could starting my career in advertising, which I meticulously planned for the last five years, be an utter source of stress? Wasn't moving alone to Cambridge at age 19 and every year to a new city more stressful than what I was doing now, settling in Zurich?

I didn't get the point. What was stress anyway? How did one quantify it, how could I compare it?

The second doctor, after asking how stressed I was, told me we should put even more things in my sensitive stomach.

We could go ahead and see what happens with a gastroscopy, but we won't do that, because it implies we put a tube down your food pipe, and that's kind of yuck.

Amazing, I wonder how *yuck* this can be compared to the daily gulp of nausea I have swallowed for the past six months.

Obviously, he has a better idea.

A therapeutic test! With little pills and a daily diary to rule things out.

That sounds absolutely swell, just like my swollen abdomen. More pills to damage my already fatigued gastric track and many more weeks if not months of mental and emotional trials in the dark.

I have clearly become allergic to nonsense.

I walk out deeply frustrated, my dad deeply despaired. *Oh, ma petite Elodie, qu'est-ce qu'il t'arrive?*[2]

I have no clue.

All I know is that I don't recognise myself. Searching for answers, going to doctors in the hope to get my health back, feeling lost and misunderstood. This was never me before.

Back in Zurich, after a visit to other specialists who made good use of the *yuck* therapy and a few months of mental support, I know what I can eat. My stomach received pills and attention to heal and my abdomen stopped feigning pregnancy.

I learnt that the repetitive use of antibiotics during my student years had damaged my stomach with a fungal infection and that my daily portions of raw fruits and vegetables were too hard for a weak digestive system.

For the first time in my healing process, I heard the term psychosomatic. I frowned, not knowing what it meant, and told myself there was no way I could be so weak. Why would my body be sick for the sake of some emotions and thoughts I wasn't even willing to feel and to consider?

Surely, one has to be psychotic to suffer from psychosomatic symptoms. Or overly sensitive.

That doesn't make sense. How could I be sensitive with such a strong mind, I thought.

I was 22 years old, two months into my first job in advertising, my body was calling and my ego bruised.

When in doubt, ask your body

> We all share similar stories of how our bodies played a major role in getting ourselves unstuck. That gives us at least a convenient place to look at.

Your body knows, whether you like it or not.

Maybe it is sensitive, maybe it is moody. For sure it is talkative.

And listening to it can become a rewarding endeavour, but for that, you need to shut up.

Not only your mouth, your brain too. All the thoughts up there. In a sense: you.

Whoever this is, you talk and think to yourself, way more than you wish to care.

All these voices, the ego, the critic, the inner child. Tall or small from its seven years, your small self graduated with honours in drama.

Your body on the other end, is maturing. Year after year, it has become wise and clever.

So clever that it embodies the qualities of an elephant.

Well, that's a compliment!

Really, it is a compliment. Elephants are beautiful and stable creatures. But even more beautiful than that, they have a reputation for remembering. And so does your body, it remembers it. All of it.

Any ache, any emotional footprint, any mental load and frustration, any unprocessed thought and unattended tension. Left to later, they linger in indifference. They turn into fear, rage or despair.

When the background noise of your thoughts and your *busy-ness* becomes too loud, your body throws the childish ruler and doer off its throne to claim its birthright: self-expression.

There is no more genuine and authentic speaker than your body to tell what you have missed and dismissed, loved and hated over the course of your life.

There is no better ally and counsellor, no better mentor and

coach for your own self, for your thoughts and for your ego, than its physical counterpart to reconnect with your true self. When your head doesn't know anymore, when it doesn't know why or what's next, your body shows it off.

And when it does, it takes the freedom to tell you all it knows from where and how it sees fit. From a busted knee to cells that throw a degenerative party, from acid reflux to skin rashes, from a stiff neck to a voice that stays still.

Oh, you will be surprised! Or clueless at first.

Fair enough.

How can you understand a language that you don't hear? How can you get around the places and messages of your body if you never travelled there?

Most likely, you haven't been discussing with anyone other than your brain lately. You weren't taught body talk at school either. There is no one to blame. It's just a fact.

Perhaps then, now is the moment to be thankful, to be humble and to observe what's happening down there.

Bowing down from the head, looking closer at yourself.

Wellbeing signs for the seeker

Signs of being unwell are signposts.

If you choose to look away,
you will hit them.

Yes they hurt,
that's what you've got them for.

Head or heart, knees or back,
hands or stomach.

Right where you placed them,
right there for you to feel yourself.

It is a girl

Well, if I wear trousers with more pockets on them,
in shades of blue, khaki and grey,

if I hang out enough with them, show that I can burp and
swear as well,

if I make boys my best friends, pretend that I can do more,

maybe then, I could become what I am not.

A boy who doesn't have to face the inner glances of self-dis-
approval. A boy who isn't judged for not helping or caring.

A boy who doesn't come across as pushy when he builds his
self-esteem.

A boy who doesn't look bitchy when he blooms out of his
childhood's body. A boy who doesn't sound preachy when he
sets his boundaries.

A boy who doesn't think twice before he dares.

Wait, I don't like to think once. When I get myself started on
thinking, I think much more than that. Perhaps a little too
much.

What if I could balance this off with feeling more? Feeling more than thinking, that should do it.

Order what you feel

If you trigger your own stress response to entertain feelings of inadequacy, if you pressure yourself to do more or act differently, if you crank yourself up to fit in arbitrary moulds, if you ache to be accepted, if you stab your being to be given the right to exist,

you place an order against yourself.

This drink is the language of your unconscious being, the emotional imprint of your wrongdoing. A biochemical cocktail of you not being who you could be, running amok in your bloodstream.

It is never tasty and always costly.

Here is your drink sir, cortisol with a dash of noradrenaline.

You may feel the rush, you may feel alert. Maybe you stand up and be fierce at your inner battle, or you crumble inside. Maybe you fight with others in the ring of your head or you rebel against your own self.

All you do there, you do to yourself.

You are your own barman, customer, drinker.

Maybe you are an addict of your wrongdoing and feeling ill already.

Maybe your body has had enough of processing and detoxifying your own mixture. It has no other choice than to leave you there. Hungover with your own choices, with aching signs to reflect on.

> You may swear, struggle and be scared. But look, your body is still there for you and it cares. It is handing you a mirror so you can stop and see yourself there.

You don't like what you see? Aren't you looking fresh and pretty? Your looks are not to blame, your body and vitality are not responsible. They are what you get for ordering what doesn't suit your being.

So, flush anything that stuffs and clogs you up.

Let your juices run happily through your veins. Let that body of yours feel happy, healthy and well hydrated.

Your taste is unique, your body is healthy.

Only when you allow it.

Crack baby, don't try

It's a baby. I find him heavy.

Six months old. How much does he weigh? Where did his parents train, to carry him around all day?

He's cute, yes. But this isn't enjoyable. I better put him back in the cradle.

There you go, slowly. Support the back of his head. That's all the attention I have, and it's outside of me.

Crack! Back to my body.

To my wrist. A nasty sound, a vivid pain.

How did I do that? Why did it happen? What is it telling me? That babies are not good for me? Obviously, they hurt my hands and compromise my yoga practice.

My wrist is taped, full of water, so said the echography.

Great timing, just before my yoga teacher training. I can't

even blame a baby. I'll just have to wrap this body part of mine and ignore another subconscious sign.

A distinct and painful crack. So is the message sent by my all-knowing subconscious, as it tries to divert me from my corporate exit. *Stay off the mat, young lady! Your heart is still burning, your brain still coping. Why don't you take a moment to rest and enjoy yourself? Just be, for a change.*

No way, says the lady. *I'm no pussy!*

My cancerous cells are out of my body. I'll show you how a stress-repented employee spreads salvation with desk yoga sessions in her soon to be funded solo-corporation!

Let me sigh at this sight.

Let her do her thing, if this is what she thinks.

She still cares so much about doing. To her, this is the only thing worth trying.

Eventually, she will tire out and rest a little further down her way.

Come in, physical wellbeing

For most of us, physical snafus mark the start of a better awareness towards our wellbeing. Before that, our wellbeing concerns are at best, oh well... inexistent.

Forgotten somewhere in a drawer, under a pile of things we bought with the promise tag *make me look happy and healthy.*

Today, they are here for you to feel, right here inside your body.

Close your eyes and take a few deep breaths, let the air flow in and out naturally. Without forcing, without judging, nor changing anything. Just let the breath come as it does.

Good.

Since we speak about wellbeing and awareness, your physical self may have used this small chance to be heard. Whenever it notices this chance – this window of awareness opening up – it uses it.

So, as you breathe naturally and focus on your body, always try to feel into it. See if you can sense any sign, any twitch or slight tension anywhere.

Thank these signs for being there, never condemn them for daring to present themselves.

Be grateful for their presence. Be curious to meet and listen.

They came because you invited them.

Get used to their presence, you are just getting started.

Your body, that bold messenger

It never gets tired to write you
wellbeing letters and to blink on
the many paths of self-deception
you are tempted to take.

From wrists that suddenly crack
to the gurgling of a rebelling stomach,
it is there to remind you, before you go
down that line and walk a little
further away from you.

Snapping at will

My right trapezius snapped at me once before.

It was the same time of the year, when the leaves shift to match my hair colour.

I visited a flatshare. Big and spacious. A majestic neighbour-hood. I would have loved to move in straight away.

The voice of reason though, said I shouldn't. The price was too proud. Four digits for a room in a shared apartment. Did I lose it? Didn't I learn to be a responsible adult, one who does the maths before she jumps on an offer?

I told myself I'd keep looking, reasoned and resigned to fall asleep. The next morning I stretched, I yawned. I did what I swore I would. I looked right and left, and *snap!*

A big jolt of pain radiated from the neck to the shoulder. A generous span of tension that would settle in immediately for a week.

No chance to keep looking in this condition.

I got the message, I accepted the flat. It was a great flatshare, the longest I ever had.

Standing tall

This is something you must have heard in a yoga class, maybe at the gym.

I've used it, written it, and repeated it everywhere I could. At the beginning of every exercise, every break, every video.

Standing tall and her best friend, *sitting tall,* have followed me faithfully for three years as I ventured with my business ideal and my cooperative self, preaching that to be well and work well, we had to feel better.

This taught me a valuable lesson. A physical point we have in common, no matter where we stand.

> Our posture, our tensions, our organs are eager to tell everything we hide about ourselves.

Some will hunch under the weight of life injunctions and show a penchant for depression.

Others will arch their body to further expose their sensitivity and missing boundaries.

Some will crank up their joints as they hold on to grudges.

Others will stiffen organs and fascia to protect unprocessed trauma.

You can read all these stories, all inside your body.

Provided that you look and listen.

So, find your own way, go on your friendly self-knowledge hunt. You will come back standing taller, feeling a little better.

Shed the shoulds off your shoulders

The shoulder drop is an exercise I've shown to corporates. I used to be one of them. I knew their pain. Their neck deserved to unstiffen.

We inhaled and raised our shoulders together. We dropped them down with everything else that wished to come along.

Big exhale through the mouth. Big sigh.

Letting down all the stress, deadlines, tough conversations. The responsibilities, thoughts and worries. All of them too much to keep on your shoulder. None of them yours to carry any further.

Work them out mentally, work them out emotionally.

And of course, work them out physically.

While we're blending all three together, how about you give yourself a mental pat on your shoulder?

Balancing ladies and gents

What if I could relax my right side for good?

What if I could stop accumulating the aches on that part of mine? Letting go of an urge to dominate myself rather than allowing who I am?

What if I could ease in, being more relaxed with what I have? Simply appreciate what is left.

Learning to receive instead of forcing to get something more, instead of going somewhere else,

where clearly, I am not to be found.

Navigating your body map

From this day onwards, consider all signs of unease as loyal markers and reminders – set by your own very personal wellbeing compass – to help you come back to yourself.

The further away you deviate from what is true to you, consciously or unconsciously, the bigger, louder, heavier and scarier your wellbeing calls will be.

From gut to art

66 *Trust your eye, trust your intuition.*
You got to just trust your gut and do what you feel is right,
and that's where the really great works come from.

David Carson[3]

If art trusts the body to make the world beautiful, maybe we can trust that art is how we work?

Where to stop

> There are experiences I can't quite explain.
> At best I can grasp them in words and
> fix them on a page. Like my trusted toes,
> marking the land from where I stand so
> that I do not forget who I am.

I am laying down. I hear this sentence clearly:

My toes are here so you remember where you stop.

I nod, I know it's true.

This is all I feel now. I feel my toes.

There, under the blanket, bundled in a pair of five, snuggling in my socks.

Why does it matter that I feel them?

I feel good. I am relaxed. I needed this. Letting my energy run freely, relaxing in my body.

Wait, where is my body?

Where did it go, the rest of me?

I'm confused, I can't reflect or think for that matter. There isn't much matter to talk about. I am a floating cloud.

Not even that. Clouds have a shape. Even that I've lost. I am a mist.

That's it, I am a warm, pleasant foggy thing that stretches horizontally.

Where I start and where I stop, how shall I know? My toes were gentle enough to give me an anchor, a red dot on the map of being. *You are here,* it says.

Thank you, very kind of you. Now I can keep wandering and enjoying the floatiness of my being a bit further.

I feel no rush, no pressure.

When did it start, when will it be over? Oh, who cares? Who dares to care?

Have you stared at the fog to define when it comes and when it dissolves? Have you tried to squeeze and seize it in your hands, like you try to seize the day and any time you can get? You don't get it, do you?

See, it's playing with you.

IN LINE

These toes right there have taught me to stop grasping for the ground. They have shown me that there was nothing my mind should try to wrap itself around.

My head was formless, as the rest of me.

I was just there, as I would always be.

A physical feeling for a whole self

Whether you call your true self
the you within – anchored down and
deep – or the higher self floating
above in some super, spiritual
or collective conscious realms.

Higher, deeper, within, above,
the location is not the point.

All this is you.

And your body is there, to let you feel it.

ON
WORKING

No appetite for SEO

How did I land there again? Listening to a keyword expert and feeling the buzz of disapproval. It gargles up from my stomach and spreads in my chest.

Relax your jaw, ma chère. There's nothing to chew on, I tell myself to calm me down. *You don't cook that way, you won't have to apply rigorously this success recipe.*

> You are a creative wonder of this world. You mix what looks good together, with a sprinkle oil and seeds on top. You are a chef of intuition, matching colours and tastes with splendour!

And you'll do the same with this keyword-thing here.

Are the two hours over yet? My loathing stare makes it to the guest speaker. Eye contact established and flash frozen. I can see she felt it.

Try something, nod, smile, just do anything. Something that tells it's not about her. How about you uncross your arms and drop your physical barrier for a second?

Just think of something else. That's right, just enjoy the feel of your body. It's here anyway. Switch your head off on your way. Here you go, a cosy turtle break.

Let's give that to her. She is doing a great job, being so ecstatic about these little words and how Google plays with them. Look how pretty, she found a way to enjoy herself while sharing expertise and passion.

You don't have to play full-on with her. You can sit back, acknowledge her contribution, note a few things down. There's no pressure.

Look at that, your shopping list is ready now! Not bad.

Here and there you'll take some of her ingredients and mix them with what's left in your communication pantry.

Oh boy, are we done?

Yes ladies, take a deep breath. We made it! I didn't even panic, didn't treat the big G names, didn't binge on caffeine and cookies.

My gaze finds its way back to her. Now softer, less judgement, more compassion. I like that.

On my emotional scale for self-inflicted terror, this feels much better.

When wellbeing doesn't work

> The issue with our current take on wellbeing is that we care when it's not there.

When it doesn't work, as you think it should. When you are in the doing, not in the being.

You have compromised it already.

And because it likes you, it will show.

Your body will. When it decides to ache to call for attention.

Your mind will. When it plays the destress, the anxious, the judge and the blasphemous.

Your account will. When it digs holes in the hope you'll stop at all costs.

Your heart will. When it feels you haven't been listening to its endless motion, not even a little beat.

Your peers will. When they are done seeing you, edited in posts.

With all the above running amok, we end up screaming for help together. We point the finger at each other.

Who gets to change first? Who gets to clean up the mess?

No one can. We're too busy working.

Roar in a keywor*l*d

Maybe I should chill.

Maybe, I will. When I see less nonsense.

We have made our versatile human beings and bodies buy into programmed beliefs. That the key to success in this world, is to express ourselves with keywords.

Keywords that satisfy algorithms and feed on biases.

Algorithms that reward crowds of followers and leave loners behind.

We voluntarily buy into it. We are the ones feeding this, any minute of our mindless browsing and scrolling.

This tenses me up.

The only way I can relax my head and ease my fingers, is to write about it. When my hands are buzzing and my jaw is tensing, I know it.

There is a blunt roar inside, worth the word fight.

So, rather than investing my physical and emotional health in the algorithm topic, I invest my thoughts, hoping you will benefit from it.

That corporations with teams of SEO experts make the consumption machine run smoothly, I didn't expect more ethics on their agenda. It says it there: keep employees and consumers *engaged* – what a word for what a world.

> But why are we – solopreneurs, business owners, repented corporate burners, disillusioned careerists, idealists and artists – playing along with this?

If we traded financial safety for freedom of work and expression already, why squeeze our valuable singularity in preselected words that fill up feeds, get more leads and stuff funnels up?

Where is freedom in this?

Where is authenticity, where is our expression?

How genuine and honest can we be, when hashtags and calls to action blur our vision?

Yes, I talk to myself, as always.

Yes, I talk to you, as we swim together in the search pond.

It is right to feel appalled at what's happening.

It is right to clench our teeth, to hold our breath for what's to come.

It is right to denounce the overwhelm and the frustration, as we work our brains out, at our computer, at our websites, at our lack of contentment for posts lacking content of their own.

It is time we step out from powerless observation.

> It is time we stop being helpless at the sight of algorithms that force to post, to work and to live on repeat, just for the sake of ranking higher than our neighbour.

It is time we ask ourselves what the heck we are doing here, tired of feeling powerless and hacked with our personal data.

To ask once and for all, who it is we are serving.

To call for change, to stop forcing ourselves to fit into moulds for the fake sake of success.

To create freedom with what we have, from where we are. With our words, our bodies, our brains and our hearts.

> If only we dare, then we care. To be free in expression more than in consumption, in moving more than in sitting, in seeing the world clearly more than staring blindly at a screen.

You can sigh, you can roll your eyes.

You can do what you want with the words I write. At least I stand up.

Standing by what I know, knowing what I feel, feeling who I am.

Aware of what can be.

Emotions with reason

How overindulgent of a wellbeing specialist, to let little words like CTA and SEO trigger such devastating emotions and mental desolation. One would think, *she should know better, she should rise higher than this low vibration.*

I know. And I know it is false.

To be as honest as I can think and feel, there is nothing I should do. And neither should you.

Let the anger come out, let it resonate through the walls of your heart and beyond.

Emotions are here for a reason, so are you.

Syndromes of a modern profession

I used to live perfectly well

before stress, distraction and procrastination

became working-world problems.

Stress
is an
existential
lie-detector
mechanism.

Stress express

Stress is what you experience whenever you agree
to something you know you don't want,

but don't dare to say.

Not even to yourself.

You would rather be in pain
than to be,

exposed to your own truth.

Distraction played well

Stop being serious, stop staring at your computer.

How long have you been there? One hour, two, three, more?

Come on, we all know and you know it too, since wellbeing at work finally made it through:

sitting for hours is no good for you.

It is no good for your back, no good for your neck, no good for your heart and arteries. It is no good for your health.

Needless to say, it is counterproductive as much as counter-intuitive.

You wonder where distractions come from?

They come from within, from the depths of your being that had enough from the never-ending waiting.

When are you going to take your limbs for a walk, your lungs for a breath and your head for a break? When are you going to care for your heart to beat and your long-forgotten child to play?

If you are lucky to be a parent, see only how long it takes for your earthling to claim your attention. How loud and expressive their despair, when they sense you don't care.

The child you once were has gone nowhere. Still sitting, still waiting impatiently, for you to see, to feel, to care, to play with itself.

It is your inner-child's job to make you stop what you're doing.

Especially if this doing makes you unwell.

Because
suffering is
widespread
in society
doesn't
make it
any less
a suffering.

Redefinitions

Suddenly I was surrounded by words that didn't make sense to me.

Distraction, procrastination, sabotage.

How could these notions create so much tension? How could mere words shatter my composure?

Yet, words are nothing. Nothing more than symptoms of the working society. Just like stress, burnout or hustling became trendy.

These are the signs of me trying too hard.

The signs of doing more than I could.

Thinking I had to become someone, because just being, obviously was not enough for me.

Avoiding another boar

I'm pounding on the bedroom floor, snoring the air in, sticking the air out.

With a tongue that long. It would scare a lion.

The biggest muscles in my body

– time for anatomy lesson? Yes, the quads! –

are on fire.

I use the hell out of them, kicking my feet as high as my eyes. Front quick, butt quick, burpee with plank rotation, flying jacks, mountain climber. And I won't stop.

I keep jumping, I keep breathing. Deep and even deeper. My head is buzzing, my sight is fogging. I could start boxing.

Where is that bear? I swear I could fight one, right now, right there.

I'd send it back to its herd, all the way up to the Uetliberg.[4]

Where is that computer? If my mind were elsewhere, I would have crushed and thrown it back to Apple.

Enough for now.

I feel a little better but my breath is still on. I jump under the shower, the water is cool.

One slow inhale. My body wants it colder. All the way to the right, ice cold for you ma'am.

I feel good, my jaw relaxes. I thank myself for taking me out of this rage.

This is what happens when I want to set up google analytics and I cannot seem to make it work.

This is what working on IT-related configurations does to my human wellbeing system.

It makes me bug, turns me into the Hulk.

My reaction illustrates the frustration, the rage and the tension when I force myself to complete tasks for which I am not suited. It's not that I'm stupid, not that I'm lazy. It's just that this thing, right there, right now, doesn't agree with me.

I concede, I can be a tad sensitive. My natural skills are closer to humanities than to machine learning. Yet, I make no false assumption when I claim that this observation is a wide-

spread phenomenon in modern corporations.

I know it is true and it rhymes.

My point is this. If you can avoid forcing yourself to waste time and build up anger on a task that doesn't work out for you, ever or at that given moment, then avoid it at all costs.

Yes, you can be stubborn and force yourself into it. Or you can stop lying to yourself and drop it.

For ever or for now. If inspiration comes and dares to help you out.

Move on. Or be ready to bruise and box another round. Your ring, your choice.

If in doubt, remember this. You are doing no one a favour walking around the office floor, like a captive boar.

Celebrate the misfit

Burnout makes you unfit to work mindlessly.

It helps you recognise you are a *misfit* in a *dysfunctional* society.

Multiply the double minus, it becomes a plus.

That makes the burn worth living.

Fun better be there

You have so much to share.

People need to know. You could start a blog and write articles. Write regularly. It is good for your website ranking, it will build your credibility. And one day who knows, you take all your posts, all your articles and make a book out of them.

Ok, I was sold. My marketing expert was right.

I executed the plan. I executed myself.

Docilely first, including SEO keywords in my titles, planting them in the first line of my articles, watering them every few sentences again.

What were they? Oh yes, always the same. *Reduce tensions, stress reduction, employee health, corporate wellbeing, increase productivity.*

After a while, I grew tired of pitching myself under the cover of what I wrote. I had to spice my prose.

Inspiration, I later remembered, only cares to come with her friend.

What was his name? Oh yes, Fun.

I regret, I see no Fun on your reservation. I see Fame, *but it hasn't arrived yet.*

How pretentious, shrugged Inspiration. *Let's go.*

Yes, Inspiration loves her dear friend.

Had I felt into my chest, I would have sensed them there, waiting for me to invite them.

OUT OF LINE

No burning, no smoking

> 66 *Je ne veux pas travailler, je ne veux pas déjeuner, je veux seulement l'oublier. Et puis, je fume.*
>
> *Sounds like Edith Piaf,*
> *but it's not* [5]

SOCIAL EMOTIONAL PHYSICAL MENTAL FINANCIAL WELLBEING

It takes a conscious effort

Take a pen and please cross the above title with me.

Take a deep breath, pen ready.

And scratch...

Ah, we feel better now, don't we?

If your being is a super-conscious and rational one, be my guest. You can hang around with that phrase and apply it thoughtfully anywhere you see fit.

But remember that,

you are welcome to scratch it out of your linear thinking head.

Whenever you are ready for it.

Minding the mingling

Some days I'd overload my social connections with wellbeing tips and offers.

I'd speak their language. Dive deep in promotion, until it felt wrong.

As wrong as extortion.

I was annoyed, why was I doing this to me?

What was there to hide, under my repetitive keywords, my misplaced calls to action?

I resolved myself, I swore. I would never sell myself again. Not until next month.

That time around, I'd go at it differently.

I'd delegate being social. I'd build a team, I'd hire someone.

Indeed, I was worth the spend.

Until I couldn't afford them.

No wonder you're feeling off

No matter how much you try to rationalise and tell yourself,

you should be working more, keep on investing in this project, stay in this team till the end.

If you're feeling off, that's enough.

It's not about the others. It's not about the situation.

It's because you are.

Your mind may be tempted to resist the feeling. Your ego may search for a better reason.

There's no need for this. Since you're feeling it, you know it already.

When I listened to myself

> The shy voice of intuition likes to repeat itself. Even if you don't listen today, even if you believe you can't afford to follow it. It will wait for you.

Mine did patiently when I was being anything but patient.

I don't want to run a business. I don't want to run after clients. I don't want to force messages into the greased wheels of search engines.

I want to feel stable and safe in my sound.

So that I can write friction free.

So that I can focus on what uplifts me.

On creating, reflecting, mirroring. On being who I am and doing what I do, when I feel myself best.

It is inside,

that I have access to those insights,

that my presence is enough,

that those who needed me, indeed found me.

Almost like every morning

I wake up with tons of energy. Start to write before I brush my teeth. I recognise the free flow of inspiration. It is almost tense and erratic. I know it is a good thing, a state full of power and ideas. Only it requires my presence to canalise it and not to undermine it.

I use the occasional and brief windows of calm to attend to my morning routine. In such moments of downloads, I do my best to let all judgements out of the way. What matters here is the information I receive, how it feels and thinks by itself as it crosses my awareness.

I take the trash out, out of compulsion, I have a shower in the middle of a sentence, I throw the rest of my coffee into the sink because it does not sit well with me.

I feel that now is the moment to update automated emails on my website and this takes me away from the story I started my day with. Something tells me it doesn't have the right angle for now. So, I go along with the other task and leave it there unfinished. A timeless zoning in acuity,[6] stopped as abruptly as it started. Lunch now has priority.

It is ready in less than five minutes. I drizzle anything that comes to mind and to my hands. According to my tastebuds, it tastes fine for that moment.

I sit down to eat, stand up three times, walk around with my plate to tidy my bedroom and prepare another coffee. Sitting down again I feel the drive to write about a chaotic morning.

I leave the unfinished plate on the side, get a toothpick and start writing, as unprocessed as possible. Describing as faithfully as I can the train of events that I chose to observe as I lived them.

I try my very best not to stand in my own way. Because of what I know, because of what I feel.

For a fact, I know it to be true. How I work does not work for you.

Efficient in existence

Moments of self-absorption is where genius happens. These moments are timeless. Because of that, they conflict with *society's* preference for you to spend more time on *making it function* and less time on *existing in it.*

Doing undisturbed

Your body gives broad way to your genius,

when you do what works for you.

If you pay attention to it when you do what you love,
you'll notice it doesn't hurt.

It doesn't disturb you. It doesn't call for another action.

It doesn't tell you that somewhat, somewhere,

there is tension in the air.

It doesn't, indeed, when there is none.

Why then, would you keep on doing and striving, when your
body keeps aching?

Welcome workholism

Workaholism is counterproductive. How about we switch to workholism?

Workaholism and workholism look similar but the latter has understood that the "a" in its core deserved a place of its own.

"a" stands for awareness. It needs space to be known. To express itself out of work and in its whole.

I know, I play with words.

I play with words to invite you to consider another, more sustainable, more respectful reality. Another approach to yourself and to the way you work. As a being, as a member of society.

You know, you – personally, socially, professionally – have been playing with words too.

Tweaking them into *seemingly true* stories that are damaging, disempowering and deceiving to your *true* nature.

A nature which, despite all this, you are still part of.

Chief Existential Officer

Being alive was the most challenging position you could get.

You should be paid for it.

Search Excuse Opinion

I choose my keywords to be different.

I give them another definition.

To remind myself that reality is what I make of it.

Reality is, after all, brought to life through language.

So, when I don't agree with the seriousness of the outer world, I take my ease, my wellbeing and myself aside.

Together we start all over again.

Again, we remember we're here to play.

If you don't enjoy working on your SEO, if you are tired of ranking for search engines and ranking for recognition, then make the letters your own.

Search for a moment.

Search inside yourself – even Google told you so.

Organise your thoughts as you wish.

Find the excuse to exist.

And reclaim your right to build a reality you feel happy with.

One you will find easily.

Don't fight what doesn't exist

If you see yourself waiting until it is forgotten or too late, be assured. It's not about you.

It's about it, not meant for you.

You may gain understanding and peace of mind from this.

Of course, you'd like to do everything you think you should.

But deep down, don't you know? If you can't get yourself to it, it's because there is something else out there. Something more in line with your flair.

You can try to beat that bad procrastination. And you'll find new ways to delay.

For I tested and failed at forcing, repeatedly. In the hustling of my entrepreneurship, in the burnout of my corporate days, in the frustration and guilt of my working patterns.

But there's another way.

You can cut yourself some slack. You can trust and procrastinate all you want.

Once you recognise the force that arises when you stop forcing. When you let yourself forget and be surprised at your true priorities.

You'll see how everything unfolds, once you give it time and space to be.

Your opportunities, if they're meant, will arise and come back to you.

They will. Once you show that you trust yourself more, than you do your to-dos.

Pro without frustration

There is a myth saying that we procrastinate.

I chose to call it *auspicious rescheduling.*

What is not meant to happen now will be dealt with later. I trust and respect my unknown timing, as I know that forcing has no benefit. All it brings is tension and frustration, where none of them needs to be.

Thoughts for a living

I couldn't take languages seriously.
Yet I went on to study communication.

I couldn't get my interest in identity.
Yet this is where inspiration found me.

I couldn't pick my brain for essays.
Yet they came back with praise.

I couldn't believe in the power of words.
Yet I use them every day to create my world.

I couldn't let myself just think for a living.
Yet this is where wellbeing takes me.

Here, have some cake with me

Ideas that spark through me are there to be shared, to be taken further, to be built upon. Especially if they contribute to something greater, if they embellish your life.

This is what I like doing. This is what it looks like.

An exchange of trust. Of mutual recognition for our beings and their individual qualities.

This is the kind of collaboration, the kind of mindset I want to foster. The kind of work ethics, the kind of culture I want to promote.

Even if I invested generously in the past, often beyond financial means. Project collaborators came on board to shine with me.

I know myself, I am fair skinned.

Too much sunlight is not good for me. Why would I expose myself for the sake of fame and recognition?

So that my skin catches on fire?

So that my pitta sharpness cranks up and makes me *krank*? [7]

So that my ego shoots in all directions and overbooks my agenda?

So that I burn myself out again?

No, I happily leave this where I found it.

At the very bottom of an aching being.

My beliefs at work

Here is an exercise you can try.

It consists in listing 50 beliefs on a certain topic. The first 20 words or phrases you will list are those of your immediate surroundings. You borrowed them from society, from your parents, from peer pressure, from the books you've read.

They sound most familiar, yet they aren't truly yours. They are those you use, to shy away from how you feel.

The more you list, the deeper you dig.

You start hearing that subtle sound, your voice beneath the ambient noise.

You realise that this you inside, knows you better than the best of your thoughts combined.

I did this exercise on *work* and *what work meant to me*. It wasn't the first time. Three years in my subconscious and wellbeing work, were still a few borrowed bits, worth unravelling.

For me, work was:
- freedom
- gain
- something new
- change
- fun
- passion
- earning
- safety
- money
- purpose
- something lovely
- one of the favourite things or mine
- something I can do anywhere
- my laptop
- my own standards
- being relaxed
- doing great things
- helping others
- inspiration

——————— THE 20 MARK

- not in an office
- making myself happy
- not what others say
- a life investment, for what?
- writing
- creating

- progress
- learning by doing
- bringing something good to others
- too much
- something else than me
- always room for opportunities
- comes easily
- collaboration
- making something new
- fascinating
- daunting
- evolution of society
- something I choose
- what I make of it
- not work
- art
- timeless
- not that important
- who needs to work?
- I don't
- not the right word to define something
  I want to love
- something I'd like to do for my own
  good
- spending time with people I respect
- learning about myself through
  projects

Wellbeing beam

It has to work, I have to make it work.

I used to think work worked that way. But it doesn't.

Call me lazy, call me arrogant, I don't mind.

That's the point. It's not about my mind. It's about my well-being.

About *what works well for me.*

If I work against my nature, my wellbeing stops me. Wellbeing goes on strike like a good Frenchman.

Since I realised I could think of anything, project it outwards and see it shine back in the world around me,

I resolved myself to let wellbeing work for me.

That's it. There is no way back.

My fuzzy stomach knows I'm right.

Ask the stars, feel my chakras.

From the root to the crown, they are buzzing and applauding at all this energy beaming in and out of me.

The works in -*ing* for my being

I see two opposite forces at work in *work*.

When I worked on something that was not meant for me, I was in a state of doing.

This doing felt like forcing. Call it striving, daring, hustling.

For a while, this seemed like the only way to be, to bring value in a society that valued masculinity.

I thought I was being a responsible adult, a professional.

I kept doing more. Like every corporate around, I collected physical warning signs.

To keep challenging myself, I then took another line. I went for an entrepreneurial round.

There, I hit the mental boundaries of wellness.

As I looked right and left, I still wasn't the only one. All of us riding the same bus to hustle, all attempting to remove blocks in the subconscious undergrounds. All trading the slow and the stable for scaling unicorns.

It didn't matter where my drive was taking me, it didn't matter which title I was using.

The more I did in the hope of becoming someone took me near the person I wanted to be.

But this wasn't me.

So, I started to question the validity of working and doing in relation to my wellbeing.

And here was the thing. When things worked out for me, I was in a state of being.

This is when I experienced effortless creation.

More and more, I chose to allow space and time for activities I enjoyed the most. I let my state of wellbeing be the start of the day, of every moment. Of every thought and every decision.

Yes, I was still tempted to grab someone else's line, just to be sure that what I felt was right and mine, just to be sure I wasn't being lazy in the eyes of others still running.

But nope.

Everything was working itself out. As long as I was letting it.

So, I kept on doing my wellbeing thing, fiddling with words and ideas. That was mine and that was fine.

For my brother, it was the driving, the prospecting, the selling.

For my mother, it was the investing, the stewing, the family gathering.

For me, it was the feeling, the reflecting, the writing.

To work without working, to journey while staying in one line with me.

How lovely, how ladylike of me!

I am sure you can think of some things ending in *-ing* that doesn't feel like working and that gets your whole being kicking. Keep them close to your heart, make them your sole priority.
These activities you enjoy, are a direct way to yourself, a way only your wellbeing can tell. As you feel and let yourself be through them, some more sparks of inspiration will take you to the next.

There again, you'll be inspired.
There again, you'll be effective in being.
There you'll have things working out,
for you and for real.

As I grew an interest in gardening, I started weeding my LinkedIn feed.

Converging lines

Reconversion in French means professional or vocational retraining.

Re*conversion* is when you allow yourself to *converge* again,

through what you feel like doing, with who you are.

66 *The bridge into a new life, repotting plants into larger and better containers quite literally grounds that person and gives him or her a sense of expansion.*

Julia Cameron [8]

Letting leaves lead your way

The world needs leaves and trees to keep nature thriving, as much as it needs racing trucks to keep society running. From where you stand, this *where* will always be your place. Anything else, outside yourself, is only passing.

Autumn leaves on the ground. My hands cupped over ginger coffee, I barely noticed them. But there they are, on either side of the street, further down my window, overlooking the river and the morning passing of people, runners and bicycles going to work.

Then comes a truck.

In the momentum, too strong to resist, the leaves seize the pull. Floating and whirling in the air, rolling and coming a few meters ahead.

How exciting, how thrilling to again be in motion. To be ready for action.

But is this truly theirs? After the passing of the moment that came to disturb their natural autumn slumber, they have come to remember that this was only a disruption, nothing to be mistaken for a reconversion.

Now, would you please walk to these autumn leaves and reprimand them for being so lazy and out of juice? Would you dare to throw your judgement at the rhythms of nature? Would you boo the golden flame of the ones once beaming in green?

You wouldn't, you don't reprimand the earth. Then why even consider reprimanding yourself?

The leaves are completely right in their being, decomposing and contributing to the ground, just as they before contributed to the tree, creating lovely shades for your beautiful eyes and breathable air for your sensitive lungs. Why think we could even argue about them?

Then why keep arguing with yourself for being you in your natural deed rather than running after the ambient momentum, suddenly whirling and passing on your LinkedIn feed?

Ok, maybe this doesn't have anything to do with you, but it sure had something to do with me.

How many times have I let myself be disturbed in my autumn leafy being? How often did the ambient social bragging expose me to unsettling uncertainties? *Maybe I, too, should do more. Roll further and better. Whirl higher and crush louder.*

Well, you know the answer. *I should* nothing.

Let the leaves be in their own right and beauty, let the trucks drive by, as fast as they will.

Maturing in intuitive work

When you find your ease, you temper your effort. The one that feels right for a fair outcome, a respectful balance of time and energy at your disposal.

This was the essence of a discussion with fellow entrepreneurs, in business for a few years.

I had so much more energy at the beginning, I had so many ideas, I wanted to change the world. Now I know what I do. I have my clients, my smaller circle and that's just right for me.

We admitted that yes, at the start, it is *fine* to strive for ideals. To move through mountains and to believe that just for a moment, we could hump and hustle to the top. Testing and failing fast, to find the fastest way back to ourselves.

At last, trusting again in the stillness of who we are, amidst those who keep running around.

It works without you

Don't get caught up, in working things out.

It's a mind trap built for an ego by another ego.

Instead, just care to get to yourself, and let all those things work themselves out.

They'll be thrilled to do that for you.

Typing in my own type

There are nights I wake up before the tram passes. The one of my own thoughts, the one outside the window, starting at five in the morning.

I get up. I try not to wake myself too much. Low light, glasses on. The only moment of the day I accept I don't see clearly. I don't need to see much when I write. What I need most then, is to not stand in my own way.

At most, I put the kettle on. Black tea and coconut milk. Unless my stomach feels queasy after the first sip. Then I switch to herbal and that's it.

Ready for output, I pour the water and the words through. They land white on black screen. I work in night mode to keep the blue light low. Night mode inside, night mode outside.

I like this time of the night, as I slowly drift to the first hours of the day. Absorbed in writing, as I transition gently from the vata realm of ideas to the comforting and stable space of kapha. The dosha switch comes at six, the next one will at ten.

Vata, kapha, pitta. I juggle with the ayurvedic doshas as they mark the phases of the day. Each dosha more or less present, in ourselves and in everything else, representing as we do, the qualities of the elements.[9]

I have a mixed constitution, predominant in pitta and vata. My pitta mind is full of fire, assertive and directive, sometimes borderline compulsive. My vata is windy, creative on most days, agitated and psychic on others.

To balance them out, I enjoy the cooling and grounding qualities of the kapha time. The moment to settle in myself, to let my ideas rest in one place, rather than stirring them further.

There they are, a bit quieter, just a little heavier, so I can grasp them and help them land on a page.

I look at the clock, maybe too often. I'd spot a 33, since I claimed this was my number.

Past nine, I open the bar for coffee.

Approaching 11, my mind is out of control. We've been in pitta time for an hour already. Enough taming, my fire is back, together with impatience.

IN LINE

My calendar tells me to *rest and digest*. Digesting goes well at this time of the day. My first window for food is between ten and two. As my mind now overacts, I know I help myself by remaining offline and quiet. I avoid emails and social media. I don't want them to feed my natural unrest.

Instead, I relax and keep it cool. Let me water plants, cook something or jump on my bicycle for a joyous ride, or a nature stroll outside.

Call my day an arranged distraction, that's alright.

I know this word doesn't apply to me. I dropped it like I dropped procrastination. Once I discovered the wonders they led me to.

Does my body feel like moving? I give it to it.

Do I sense a craving for intermittent cooking? Let me taste it.

Is my mind in the mood for browsing? Let her teach me something.

I have always found solutions and revelations, missing parts of a puzzle in little moments of exploration. They may seem chaotic and random, it doesn't make them any less valuable.

What's the pathos all about?

My mind likes to play as if it were distracted, but it never is.

It is connected.

There comes an insightful message between the lines. There I remember I have an observation to spare. Inspired, confident and aware. Gently driven by my own and best self.

IN LINE

Dancing briefcase

The world would be more fun,

if policy makers and board members were moving more, when talking rules and numbers.

Observing
the efficient

Hours after noon, I gazed in the void of the television.

My brother and my cousin playing videogames, this was the stage for my homework. Not at a desk, not in my room. Nested in the sofa, with piles of paper spread around, while space troopers were sent on missions, while cars were pimped in colours.

It was the perfect time to doze out, to experience my first meditative states. Emptying my mind from hyperactive thoughts, letting the stream of images wash over my otherwise sensitive screen.

In these moments I felt quiet, at peace and confident.

I knew I was far from being focused. Still, I didn't doubt I was efficient. I knew I had all the right to stay, in this mentally relaxing, in this emotionally soothing state, for as long as I wanted.

A jolt of inspiration and it would be the start of a new realisation.

Good
time to
remember,
there's no
such thing as
procrastination.

Earning as you are

I do not believe in working hard nor hustling. I believe in earning differently. I believe in winning every day.

Being in line and in balance, in every wellbeing account.

Playing again with yourself

> When life, work, and play
> exist all at once,
> you exist
> to the best of your expression.

Remember yourself as a child, playfulness has gone astray since then.

Still, it is there. If you choose to call it forth.

It comes from within. Up to you to decide, when to bring it back, any moment of your life.

To be in the direct experience of it, no matter the circumstance, no matter the ambient pressure.

I am doing it now as I write, I am absorbed.

I am free to express any idea. Happy to share whatever comes through. Open to see where this leads me to.

Without any should and must, without any picture of what shall come out.

There, in that state, on the playground table I call my house, I can be truly generous.

Generous with myself.

Generous with my time, with my presence, with my existence.

And from this place, word after word, I am mesmerised.

How easily this came to be. How wholeheartedly, life offered again, to play with me.

Once and for all, everyone is perfect

Nobody is perfect is an idiomatic nonsense. If you were to see how everything you are being right now is perfect, then *now* would be a much more enjoyable and relaxing place to be.

You are in the perfect place and in the perfect state for your own sake. Every single moment of it.

Even if you coin yourself a perfectionist.

Perfectionism has a bad reputation. But in and of itself, it is a state of being perfect, more than one of inefficiency.

Being a perfectionist – the way we're used to use it – is a limited judgement, to dismiss who you are and what you enjoy doing, in your otherwise best and most-suited element.

It is a misconception, a pressure to work faster, on tasks you don't like.

But what about those other tasks you like? The ones that like you back?

What if what you do, were a passion of yours?

What if perfection then, were a simple translation of your ability to excel.

What if your ability to dive deep, to forget time and yourself in that action, were the right space and state, for you to be?

The one in which your thoughts wander and your question finds an answer.

What then, makes perfection different from meditation?

What if these were the moments your brain needed, to switch off really and remain quiet consciously?

To leave space for the silent you to have a say?

Perfection
is the
closest
you get,
to being
yourself.

Start once
I spark

I have talked with the publisher and
the designer of this book before I had
5% of it written. I have trusted projects
and visions before I had a reason. The
feeling of an idea is enough. As I sense
the spark of excitement in myself and
others, I know life will deliver.

Best project ever

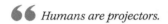 *Humans are projectors.*

The basic movement of the human psyche is projection. So, we have to project it in order to see it ourselves.

Projection is the dynamic that allows consciousness.

You cannot project something that doesn't exist in you to some degree.

Every person's projection of the divine is actually a reflection of the presence of the divine in them.

The human being is the microcosm of the macrocosm.

Humans have this spark of the divine. The spirit in one's life. Jung called it the Self. The Romans called it the Genius.

Everybody has that.

Michael J. Meade [10]

Alright then, it's time you project your uncompromised self, your genius out there. So that you may see how great of a job you're doing at being.

You is the only thing you can project, the best project you'll ever work on.

ON BEING
SOME ONE

Passing among the signs

After years of stomach aches and allergies, attributed to a job in advertising – or was it a relationship? – I was cured for a while.

Then, on I went.

Other companies, other relations. Other stories, other symptoms. Still not fulfilled, still not fully me.

A lockjaw to chew on and precancerous cells to sit on, all set for another transition.

Resignation, separation, operation.

By then, burnout made it to an occupational phenomenon.[11] I was carrying its symptoms around, as I behaved every day. I didn't recognise them in me, didn't recognise myself anyway.

Overachiever, a tad cynical, and insecure for sure.
How bad could this be? Didn't every founder and co-worker around, run on pressure steam like me?

Three years in my solo company, I had consumed myself slow and steady. Rare when I started, medium well by the time I startled, upon writing these lines.

> My signs of being unwell all came and went. Each in their season and flavour, each craving the scattered attention of their stubborn maker.

Kintsugi fix

I am tired. I have burnt out. Even though I can't believe I have.

I changed so much.

Jobs, friends, haircuts.

I resigned. I left the industry.

I broke up. Once, twice, three times.

I changed flats. I moved out, and out, and out again.

I cut myself short, let myself grow.

I have moved on. Certainly, I was still broken inside.

Can someone pass me some gold?

So I can fix myself, like a work of kintsugi.

Hold on a second. Gold I can't afford.

Yes, I varied the signs of being unwell, for better combustion and more confusion.

More than F-ed up

We have different ways to process reality.

If we can't discuss it openly, we notice at least when we disagree.

What difference does it make?

If you're an F or a T?[12]

If you do a personality test in the hope to understand yourself better, then you know what it is

to be reduced to letters.

Between the Feeling and the Thinking types, I do both.

I am T-ied up to the limits of thinking.

F-ed up from feeling too much. Being of that kind, I apparently do this, more extensively.

I know what they say, these are tendencies. Not to be taken

too seriously. And wait, there are four more to go. INFP-A. Now I shall be complete.

Very handy, the language, the test, the code, when it comes to separating one from another.

Thinking that since we built a proof with studies and research, we can camp on differences without asking further, without digging deeper,

for who we are beneath a letter.

The you(s) is your head

What is your relation to you? Wait a moment, who is the *you* I talk about?

You in your body or you inside your mind?

Your self-constructed identity, the one you drive around in your brand-new car or the one you wrap in sustainable clothes?

The one who rests down below or the one you project in your projects?

The one who runs from meeting to meeting or the one who shines on LinkedIn?

The forgotten self, written in small, or the mighty Self in capital? The one who makes the laws in your country or the one who goes on to break them?

Who am I talking about? I don't know, I am not in your head. But since you must be as human as me, I think we can both agree, the inhabitants inside you are more than one. That's all I invite you to reckon.

Told myself so

What I tell myself and what I do, even in the smallest words and actions, set the clear lines for my wellbeing.

They tell me where I am, they show what works and what doens't for me.

There's no way to trespass them. No way to ignore or change their course.

If my thoughts and feelings are against me, the lines I follow lead away from me.

No running away

Do you go for a run in someone else's running shoes?

You don't.

Then why embark on a new job, when you stand besides your shoes?

Why step further and commit any longer?

A relationship, a venture, an adventure, whatever the nature.

Why go for some *thing* or some *one* when you are besides your *self*?

How are you supposed to feel? How are you likely to look?

Running on the asphalt barefoot.

Fast forward. You are dreading it, maybe you hide it. But it shows. And it hurts.

It hurts your body. It hurts your buddies. It hurts your life.

Look where you stand now. Look at your feet, that first step where it all began.

Dotted potentials

I used to bump myself in doors and tables, any piece of furniture I could find for that matter.

This never made much sense. I am a petite, composed and gracious being.

Still, I'd manage to hit myself physically, as I did figuratively,

trying to fit in places that weren't meant for me.

Stuck in being

If feeling stuck, clueless, unwell or uncomfortable best defines where you are now, please be assured and reassured, this stage won't last forever.

If you don't know how you feel, don't worry. This too will change.

Don't worry about the details of your current situation.

If you are still on fire in corporate, if you work like a hamster in your home office.

If you are self-employed, if you call yourself your own boss or are free from them altogether.

If you dared to leave everyone behind to express your artistic self, if you are back again for a part-, full-, flex-, or god knows what this time.

Why care so much about the details of what you do?

Why not just care about being you?

Each to their line

> I have my way of being, you have yours.
> I have my wellbeing lines, you have your
> own. If I mix up my way of being for yours,
> if I cruise through life on a line that's not
> mine, that's where my wellbeing starts to
> blink and blind.

Yes, the blinking is annoying, often confusing, but it is here to help. To catch your attention. To show you that the thing you're pursuing isn't yours. To tell you that the other thing you're running away from,

is you.

Whatever road you're on, whatever keeps your mind up at night and your body numb at day.

Be aware of the signs, your wellbeing was made to shine.

 OUT OF LINE

To explore further

Plant or alternative, western or eastern, augmented reality or new earth. There are countless lines of research to take you further and yet much closer.

From massage therapists to somatic bodyworkers, from mentors to energy healers, there is no shortage of individuals who will embark on a wellbeing exploration with you. To help you feel and find your way.

Some have been there to help from the start, others have left their previous rat-race jobs and career tags to devote themselves to your wellbeing, once or while they were figuring theirs out.

Let your *distracted* – hmm *connected* – mind wonder. Follow it where it leads you. To the words of your neighbour, to the lyrics of that song.

Let yourself travel to the world of organs and emotions.

To the lands of wounded and healed-ever-after male and female energies.

Whatever blinks on your wellbeing plate, reach out, be curious. If this feels right and inspiring to you, not because you believe you have to.

There is so much to explore, so much to uncover, provided you are ready for a real encounter. With a self with as many questions as there are answers.

Is this wellbeing thing for you?

To answer this, you need to know who you are.

If I ask who I am on the surface, it keeps changing and makes me a prone to borderline personality disorder. But at the core, it is one big and steady stream of knowing.

The idea that I have of you on the surface, dear reader, shares many traits with me.

If I were to make your portrait through mirrored experience, using hashtags instead of strokes, we would follow each other like this:

#corporatelife #overachiever #empath #findyourwhy
#careergoals #burnoutsupport #feelingstuck
#intransition #yogateachertraining #selfacceptance
#solopreneur #imposteursyndrome #startuplife
#sidehustle #procrastination #mentalheathmatters
#breathe #homeofficegoals #timetoswitchoff
#opentowork #actuallyno

I know we've hashtaged ourselves along these lines to tell all about our lives. So much so it feels like we're playing bingo.

But the words you use to define yourself shall not outweigh the importance of your wellbeing.

> Your wellbeing is formless, nameless, not bound to external conditions, not determined by a popular hashtag.

Your wellbeing only has one tag, with *you* on it.

So, I invite you to care less about the names you've been calling yourself, to care more about being the person you feel you are instead.

What is there to be once you drop all the names that make you feel any less than yourself?

Making space for the bad

Miles of stumbling upon the lines of my wellbeing have shown me, everything I ever felt, had the right to be said.

Everything I was, good and bad, acceptable and negotiable, had the right to exist.

Every experience I made, had the right to be shared.

As an example, as an expression of where wellbeing lines have taken me.

Yes, I have been in suboptimal states.

I still feel the unease when I see them written in these lines here.

But I chose to let my dark corners find space on a page.

I chose not to dismiss them, not to dismiss myself.

To be open and honest instead.

Who knows, if we allow ourselves to
show more of what we are, including the
unacceptable and the questionable, perhaps
we can come to terms with ourselves.
With humbler egos. No matter how bruised
they are.

Deviation to the self

Is there any shortcut to harnessing the potential of your well-being for your own sake?

No, it is a live-streamed work in progress.

There is no fast forward in your hero's journey. The only way to come back to yourself, with understanding and hindsight, is to go away.

Go on your ride without a wait. Go up and down, straight and sideways.

Get stuck and pause occasionally.

Grow tired of trying and searching.

Lose yourself on repeat and marvel at the complex beauty of a regained life in simplicity.

You come back to yourself ultimately.

Total yet humble. Richer yet simpler.

Same as before but feeling complete and that is the difference.

Wellbeing is only sustainable when cultivated by and for the same person.

Wellbeing times

My mental health was lost in its wanderings. Somewhere far, far away from me.

There I was indeed, not enjoying my own company.

My ego kept pulling the blanket to itself, I whined cold in a corner of the bed.

Because I adventured so far from who I was by sticking to a busyness without a plan, I faced another challenge.

The way back, I feared, would be the greater stretch.

But wellbeing lines are not like that.

They are forgiving and non-linear. Like our good old relatives, space and time.

You are here.
First for
yourself, then
for others.
This matters
more than
anything you
think you do.

Lessons waiting in line

Slow down. There are lessons in everything you do. I find lessons in bicycle rides, in fruits that I eat.

To see where yours are, you have all your attention.

It begins with an invitation

You, yourself.

You and your wellbeing are an invitation to be seized, to help you lead a life which is more enjoyable, more respectful, more natural and in line with you.

If you have lost yourself on the way, between the insides and out – the career and education, the self-development and transition – don't worry, there's a thin line you'll find, marking where you start and where you stop.

A line made just for you. A line made to stumble on a few times.

If your wellbeing has any guidelines, that's the only one you have.

Unwrap yourself

A wise and white-bearded man[13] once said,

the word *entwickeln,* when you split it after *ent,*

means that you *unwrap,* rather than *develop* yourself.

Self-*de-velopment* then, is the act of *un-wrapping* who you are. There's nothing more to add.

I believe this to be more accurate and beneficial existentially. Even if it isn't pleasing to a consumer society.

Who needs more layers of knowledge, of information, of understanding, of roles and identities on a self who suffocates already?

So, how about you *de-velop* yourself?

How about you strip away those layers to uncover who is left there, under your constructed and consumed self?

Well
identified

Limitations to my wellbeing are in self-definition.

When I cling to an identity, to an occupation,

to a brand, to a role, a life, a realisation.

They may mean well for me,

and just as well, not be meant any longer.

Better gifted than encrypted

 *There are 2 basic views of the nature of the soul.*

One is that the soul is empty, you come in empty and the world writes on you, family writes on you, your neighbourhood writes on you, school writes on you and you become the sum of experiences written on you.

That seems to be the modern idea.

The ancient idea found throughout the world is every soul comes into the world

as a unique essence that has its own gifts to give,

and qualities and capacities to experience.

And each person is here on earth to awaken to that inner conglomeration of gifts and capacities, aims and purposes.

That's what we're here to do and that got forgotten.

Michael J. Meade [14]

Being is
beyond
understanding.
So, don't wait
to be
understood
to be yourself.

Take the same and shed again

The art of transition, what a beautiful thing. Shedding the old for the new without looking back. If you need physical help with that, a torticollis will.

Yes, it hurts to walk away, to leave your cocoon busted open in a mess.

How do you dare fly away feeling lighter, to let nature clean up after you left?

Why feel guilty, why feel sorry? You took one step further on your natural evolution.

Who dares blame you for that?

Would you talk down at a butterfly,

for colouring your day with painted wings, when this day is the only one it gets to live?

Would you summon its unique pattern for scaring the insect world?

You wouldn't. And if you did, you must be an angry bird.

Stop holding yourself accountable for the beauty your progress brings about.

You are an inspiration in action.

This is how much leadership course you need. It is yours and it is free.

Stop feeling sorry for your fellow rampants who are painfully cocooning. It is necessary and part of the process, as heartbreaking as it may seem to you.

You have just been there a day ago. And today you are here.

They too, will shed their load,

if and when their time comes.

If and when they want so.

Showing
who you are or
pretending you
are someone
requires the
same amount
of energy.
Between being
and faking, you
get to choose.

Follow
your lead

What we need is life leadership. The one that we ought to cultivate for ourselves first, each to our own. Collectively then, we can inspire each other as the genuine expression of who we are. Being well at being ourselves. Without telling a neighbour to be better than another.

Being in-different

We may be different.

If this is what we have in common,

Can we stop beating ourselves up for being different?

Different from what?

If we are all different,

there is no norm.

If there is no norm,

there is no space for *differences* in being different.

Then there is only space for being.

IN LINE

Floating home

Whenever you decide to come again to yourself, change happens.

As instant as a snap, as immediate as a wellbeing ping. Waiting for you to take a ride with them. Waiting for you to lift that gleaming finger of yours and call home. Yes, just like E.T. on his flying bicycle. Hop on and snug in the basket under your wellbeing blanket.

You don't have to know *how*. The *how* takes care of itself, it brings you where you need to be.

When you run your life in line with your being, your world runs itself.

All ready complete

I don't have to *do* anything to *feel* that I am *being* unique.

Unique, since individual.

Indivisible, since complete.

Completely true with no effort.

And what if, after all, you didn't have to be someone?

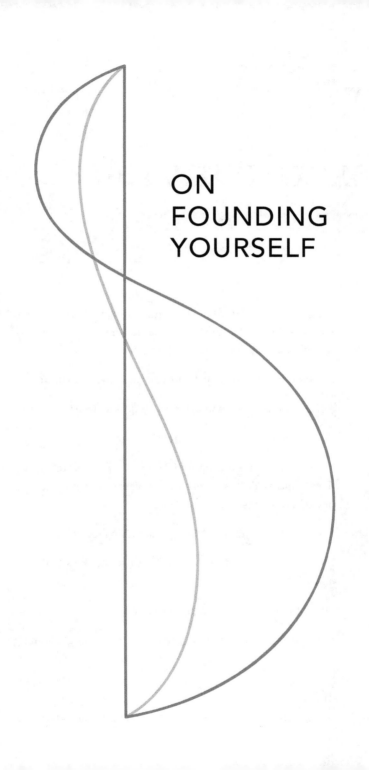

ON
FOUNDING
YOURSELF

Excuse myself in my bubble

Does he realise he told me this story already? Maybe he told it differently, but I know it is the same. This one and most of the others. Why does he keep doing that?

Am I too polite? Too considerate to hide my confusion?

At least, I must look bored. Or do I hide it so well?

Oh boy. How did we end up there?

Seven years of friendship and I don't have much to say. He doesn't either. Still, he keeps the conversation going. At least one of us shows some motivation.

How can I say what I feel without sounding ungrateful?

I feel sad for us. Sad, restless, and stuck. Stuck as I sit here and sip my tea.

I used to love this café. Right now, I hate it.

I used to love hanging out. Brunching, munching, planning

lunches to familiar and unknown places. Strolling through towns and museums, on sunny and rainy days.

I have changed. He hasn't.

Who is there to fault?

I became allergic to old stories from the ad industry. And so? I moved on to the startup community. I have new priorities. I am hustling now! Far better than running after deadlines.

My lifestyle, too, has changed. I have no time left to spend on city outings. Let alone any money.

Hmm, really?

Yes, I invest every penny on snacks and coffee. I call this co-working.

How about my evenings?

I'm overbooked. Networking and hacking myself lean.

I became a serial networker, a blind opportunity seeker, an avid lead generator.

And a lousy friend.

How could I give up my old friendship so easily? The one which made me feel *dihei in Züri*?[15]

My lip bubbles up as I sense my inner fury. Since when do I blister in the blink of an encounter?

If my body revolts to my social status, perhaps I should update it.

New busyness, new world, new operating system, new folks.

Ok, now I feel entitled to go, guilty or not. Because my body told me so.

Fooling out

Get yourself out there is the phrase that fuels and fools. While you are out there, who is left, alone and unattended, inside yourself?

Flapping to land somewhere

After years in advertising, I freelanced and translated slogans. I liked the freedom. I liked that it included writing, it allowed me to be free and fussy about language.

Officially, my next career step from there was a PhD in consumer psychology. I found my supervisor, my research topic and the university of Vienna to back me. All I needed was a side job in Zurich, to pay the bills. Part-time researching, part-time working.

But in my daydreams of the spring, I was already gone. My mind took me elsewhere in Asia. There, I'd see myself doing a yoga teacher training. Alright, very om and fancy... first, complete that PhD.

Why would I wait though?

I went to India. Once, twice, three times. Coming back to Zurich, I started offering yoga sessions to former advertising colleagues. I forgot the research, forgot to look for a job, forgot all about the bills.

There I was, building a brand in my sole company, on the benches of a cemetery. I started networking and immersed myself in corporate wellbeing.

What a bird... thought my advisor at the unemployment office. The kind that flew away constantly. The kind you'd throw out of the nest, up in the air, broken wing or not.

I would land a couple miles away from where I'd intended. Running a wellbeing business without a plan, as long as I kept flapping.

Almost had it, almost knew it

It didn't cross my mind that I burnt out in advertising. I would always say, I *almost* had one.

Almost. But not quite. This was more acceptable.

Yes, I underwent surgery. But I recovered well and fast, physically.

I was ready for the next round. Ready to shove the signs of my unwell to another square.

I took my physical health and my pumped ego with me. Carried them out of advertising and reinvested my pains and disbeliefs in corporate wellbeing.

I was a solopreneur. Independent at last, free to invest more than I had.

More time, more money.

I favoured my business network over personal bonds. My friends didn't see much of me. I didn't see myself either.

My body was healthier than ever. My stamina was arrogant and louder than my account blinker. Red in the social, red in the bank.

What was that flashing all about?

Glad I asked!

My unwell was ready to take me somewhere else. *How about we go mental this time around?*

 OUT OF LINE

Burnout burnt down

Burnout is a self-orchestrated scam we do to ourselves in a last attempt to burn down every aspect of our misconstructed self.

It is an internal call for awareness. A chance, at last, to rest and reset.

To recognise and respect that the person who burnt,

was no one,

compared to the being who had to be felt inside.

Lacking substance

I was harsh on myself.

Whatever I did, I was lacking substance.

Eventually, I got some.

A drop on a piece of paper.

More powder to rub with my finger.

Pills of shapes and colour neatly pressed together.

With them I gained in depth. I went overboard, travelled to new dimensions.

There was indeed so much more to me,

that matter and reason couldn't see.

Starting to miss the point

As I dived in entrepreneurship, I swam with idealists and other business owners. We had a lot in common.

We had gone through and beyond corporate-induced physical aches. We sought out the hell of ourselves, to create something better for others.

We tippy-toed in the snow, swam in freezing rivers to keep our mind and blood cool.

We stood up at six on Monday mornings, for accountability meetings and pomodoro sprints.

We dashed frantically drops of lemon essential oil in cascara tea, to maximise productivity.

We took deep dives in subconscious waters with rapid transformational therapy. Not for the love and curiosity of ourselves, but to debunk whatever blocked our businesses, to shed feelings of inadequacy.

As I kept hacking myself, straining my attention on conversion funnels and unconscious tunnels, I went all the way. Ending up deeper and further than I started.

Going mental in wellbeing

I never considered myself anxious, I never thought I was mental.

Until three years in my entrepreneurial journey.

Once I braved the mysteries of psychosomatic symptoms in my physical body.

Once I declared loud and clear, that I was not emotionally weak but highly sensitive equipped.

Once I cut myself from social ties, so I could scale fast and free.

Once I lost the weight of capital safety, through many rounds of unsavvy bootstrappery.

There I was, in the Lean In circle[16] I co-started and called *Leading to Wellbeing in Business*.

Wrapping *wellbeing* tight, between *leading* and *business*.

Adding some makeup to make wellbeing more acceptable in my eyes.

Because simply on its own, *wellbeing* wasn't enough.

Thanks to its members, the circle became a space I could visit and nurture for self-therapy. From my manic visions to my depressive trips, from self-judgement to little acceptance, I slowly shed the mental weight at the base of my wellbeing business.

Together, we shared our experiences, we discussed burnouts in past and present tenses. Simply, we took time for ourselves.

Together we created the space we wanted, the one I needed. A place simply called Lean In *Wellbeing*.

Hide and seek for so long

My favourite game until recently was
hide and seek. As I reached my 33rd
year, I relaxed and stopped counting.
I used to be my best critic, an eager life
seeker. I took my game too seriously.
Exploring the isolated lands and
darkest caves of my own territory.
Looking always further,

I found what I was searching.

The shortest way back to myself.

Treating wealth well

Even though I stretched myself as a yogi, even though I played the artist card. Why would I jeopardise my wealth while I worshiped my health?

Idealist or not, I deserved conscious care.

Capitalist or not, I deserved a comfy cushion.

Being with accountability

The highs and lows of my bank accounts are no different than the fluctuations of my social capital. Dent after dent, they follow the curves of my emotional and mental balance.

I remember when I juggled with available funds, when I invested many thousands.

More than what I had. Since who I was, was not enough.

Investing my energy in being busy, in getting better at doing, in doing more so I could be someone.

> Money, like buddies and body aches, comes and goes with lessons.

Finances speak a symptomatic language. The one you use today, the one you grew up with. The one of lack and worry. The one of trust and generosity.

Listen closely. Make yourself accountable.

See what takes it high. Watch out for what brings it low.

Your balance is always there, precisely where you left yourself.

Leave the seat in the stadium

The stadium pitch, the one of a kind, was presented by Chet Holmes in his generously oiled *Sales Machine*.[17]

Imagine a stadium and assume that for any service or product in any industry, at any given moment, 90% of your audience is ready to leave the minute you open your mouth.

The first third *know they aren't interested* in what you have to say. The other third *think they aren't interest.* The last third simply *doesn't think* about it.

It leaves you with 10%. Seven of which are open but not actively looking for what you have. And three, at last, could buy.

I welcomed the compelling insights and applied them to my busy-doing. I worked on my core story, dug for data from the *badi*.[18] I was determined to find facts that would glue spectators to their seats no matter which tier they sat in. This way I thought, they would never dare to leave me, all alone in my stadium.

How desperate, how manipulative.

And fair enough, my body wouldn't let me. Exit signs started to blink right and left. Sirens of my subconscious spotted a fire. Myself first, I was ready to desert the stage.

Even if I had rented that damn place for the day. Even if I had bootstrapped at will and posted on purpose to gather a such a rich crowd of leads. I still couldn't do that to myself. It still felt off. It still was a trap.

For me and for them.

When did we reach this point? When did we convince ourselves that pitching for more consumption was what we wanted?

When did we get a plastic seat glued to our rear? When did we become disable to escape from our consumer cages?

When did we lose our free will, our knowing, our integrity? Claiming we didn't need this today and waiting in line for it tomorrow?

> How are we supposed to trust our judgement, when all we see are ads with more reasons to believe them and better doubt ourselves? Is this how I want to share wellbeing and show that I care?

> Is this worth a stadium with my brand and my ego on a pedestal, just so that I can start a human conversation?

My body closes, my consciousness knows better, my reason follows.

I'm out, same way as I came in. With a free pitch for everyone. One of freedom.

Get out of here!

Call it sabotage, call it procrastination, call it quitting. I don't give a ticket.

All I give, is a damn. I give a deep and true damn about how I feel.

And I want you to give a damn about how you feel too.

So, stand up, walk out, leave every stadium you ever entered until you can walk around, strong and stable, like your own living stadium. Filled up with self-respect and love, from the toes to the top, feeling certain of who you are, thinking for yourself and yourself only. Whatever it is you truly desire.

Connectivity switch

I can hear music in the distance. Where does it come from, who switched it on? I turn around.

Now I know. Outside the door.

I push the blankets and sit up. Put my hand on the floor next to my hips, whirl over to a soft plank, walk my feet up to my hands. Forward fold. I bend the knees gently, kiss my nose *good morning* with my shins and roll up slowly.

A weird flow to start the day but this is how I stand.

Feet in the slippers, I hush out of my room. I take my phone to switch off the alarm and leave it on the table. Next to Ganesha and one of the monkeys. I don't know which one it is. If it hides its eyes, mouth, or ears. Or nothing, it just sits there and chills. It is golden and guards the entrance with its trumped-goded-friend.

Morning duties completed, I fold my mattress in three. I get myself a drink. Plain water first, followed by a long series of teas.

I sip and sit, with my computer ready to roll in night time

mode. My phone is, where did I leave it? Right, in the golden hall.

I used to need it to work. Not anymore. All that time wasted, only to share a hotspot with myself, between *Handy* and *Compi*.[19] All that because I thought I couldn't afford to get Wi-Fi.

Hotspot, 4G, 5G, what difference does it make? All these mornings and moments wasted, in search of connectivity. Refreshing my networks in the hope that Elodie's iPhone would finally appear.

How many thoughts went through my mind as I carved the belief that I didn't have enough?

Obviously, I wasn't good enough at handling the little money I had. How could I take on even more? More responsibility for yet another bill.

How many client calls did I compromise in the name of scarcity? How often did this come back to me, with a slap on my cheek?

More judgement, more inadequacy, deeper dents.

How could I pretend to be self-worthy, with all these thoughts and small actions repeated daily against me?

On and off again. I don't need another G.

What I need is that fine connection with myself.

When I am
offline,
I am in line
with who I am.

Content containing lobster

Discontentment is a good sign, it is a call for a new home.

It tells you that your job, your situation, your beliefs, the reality you live in,

cannot contain your mighty anymore.

There is nothing to resent in the process,

no reason to stay in a snug discomfort any longer.

Rejoice, you have outgrown yourself!

Go find a place in a corner, like your friend the lobster.

Find that shelter where you are safe to shed the old, and grow yourself a new container.

Compulsive understanding

I eventually got the message. Selling myself, wasn't what I wanted.

This must have been someone else's line I was trying to ride. Certainly not mine.

I was better where I was now, better at other things too. Thinking, observing, writing.

With compulsive inspiration, my wellbeing rewarded me. Good news then, we seemed to agree.

Reflecting against my mirrors

Everywhere I go, I hold a mirror to myself.

I live on my own as I interact with the world. I experience what triggers me in others.

Sometimes I get carried away, I react. Only to sit back later and reflect on what happened.

And again, I remember this was not about them. It was about me.

It always is.

Anything that happens outside of me is a reflection on what I tell myself, deep inside.

Unattended business, dis-functional relations, disproportional expectations, unexpressed emotions.

There they are, right where they were born.

In you and me respectively, for you and me to see.

Cold shower

I took the habit of taking cold showers. It is like coming to life, knowing very well what I signed up for. As I breathe deeper, I remember that I can sustain myself, no matter the weather.

Calling colder

While entrepreneurs knocked on doors to collect more *no's* and reach a small percentage of those who'd say *yes*, I didn't bother much.

According to the judge inside me, never enough.

According to my guilty feelings, alright... I'd try. Only for a while.

Just some more to make some noise. Loud enough to annoy my neighbours.

Until someone, somewhere, would dial my number and ask for an offer.

 ALONG THE LINE

Running
in the dark

Just like the wee mornings in the
Japanese farmland, my business gave
me the courage to rise up from the
ground. Stepping in the dark, tippy-
toeing in one-size-fits-all slippers,
groping my way along walls of paper.
Even if tedious at times, the memory
of my run after all, was kind of fun.

Growth mindset

Growing is great.
Growing in the direction mapped
by your nature,
naturally works best.

Yet we cookie-cut ourselves, shape appearance to match the world's demands. We biohack ourselves, play with science to master mother nature.

My father grafted trees. He too, wanted to tweak his life. He wanted to have a say, life should look and taste his way.

Branching to the side

On a New Year's walk to a Shinto temple, I adventured to the back of the shrine where I found rows of sturdy tall trees. Between them stood one of another kind. It was short, with a panoply of broad branches reaching in all directions. The further to the sides, the better.

And I told myself, if only I, as the other trees, had used my matter and energy to grow tall and straight, I would have also reached success and stable finances in my business by now.

I blinked at the judgemental non-sense I'd uttered. What kind of tree in its natural right would care about growing the same way as another kind?

These were not the same trees. They were plants with their own plans.

The unique tree in the middle looked funny and smaller, because isolated in a sea of homogenous others.

Yes, it was on its own. And it kept starring its own qualities.

Beautiful and generous with its umbrella-like horizontal reach. Playful and inventive considering all the directions its branches could explore. One of a kind, no matter which kind it was.

This helped me realise that amidst the forest of professionals and business owners who either followed a modernised ladder to climb up and consciously laid their steps for success, I was hopping from one stone to the next. I was dancing on Japanese garden steps.

No clear road for execution. No business plan for me.

I branched out where inspiration invited me. I gathered insights, learnings, sparks and wonders of all sorts.

Obviously to fill in the blank pages of a book. Doing and being my own thing.

What a thing I was, I didn't know. I guessed rebellious to others, faithful to myself.

Even though at that moment, I had forgotten where I was heading, I knew by looking at this one tree, I could trust again.

There was nothing worth doing against myself, I would keep on being me, in complete difference.

Imposter what?

I started to run a corporate wellbeing business (my imposter *what*) to help people use their wellbeing to work less and live more, in line with themselves (my *why*). I then noticed that I was imposting at imposing myself to run a business. So, I traded my *what* for another *what*. I allowed myself to write a book (another *what*) about my *why* instead.

The founder therapy

You can spend your life in therapy.

Or you can start a business for any reason that fits into a big why. And be told that in each person, there is a book worth being written.

I took the founder and writer route.

It was exciting to live, almost less stigmatising to experience.

It gave me something to create, a reason to be known for.

The reason to know myself more.

IN LINE

Art for business

The industry needs poetry

A stoic guide for corporate dropout

A philosopher for entrepreneur

A rupi kaur for hustler

The beauty of service

You have a beautiful service, Elodie. It is smooth, round, elegant. But I don't get your strategy.

These were the words of my tennis coach.

It was simple, I didn't have a strategy.

It still is today, I wouldn't need one.

A simple life is complex enough

Life can be simple, if I choose it.

I had this potential to live a quieter life all that time, available and waiting for me.

All I had to get it, was to allow it.

Enough forcing and wasting. Enough pushing and hustling out there.

I slowed and stepped down. Reduced my time online and capitalised my time off.

I shrunk living costs and commitments. Traded entitlement for enjoyment.

I refused zoom meetings and took on grannysitting. For my peace of mind and kindness of heart.

❝ With each person who makes the journey, the journey becomes more familiar and doable for each one of us.

Nusra Sahin[20]

Entrepreneur-
ship was the
most accepted
path I could
take, for what
in reality, was
a spiritual
undertaking.

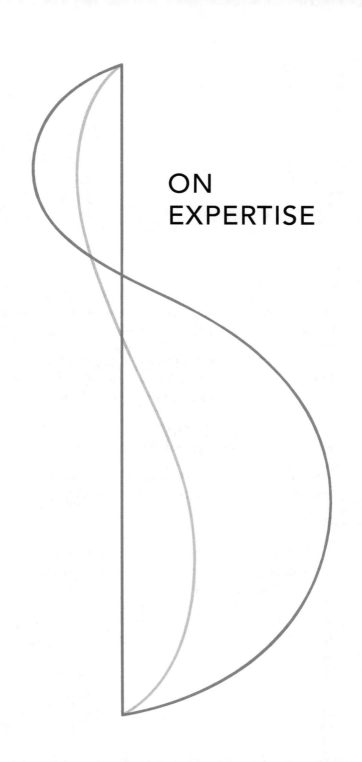

ON
EXPERTISE

Ping to being well

What am I doing here sitting at my desk, when I tell you, you shouldn't be doing this? Not like me, not hours at a stretch.

Why would I want you to breathe and stretch for the sake of work health and productivity? Because I struggle with it, doesn't mean I should crusade for it.

Why did I make this an 'expertise' of mine? I'd rather be standing up now, show myself I can take a break anytime.

Why would I even care about corporate wellbeing? Was that the best excuse I found, to better care for myself?

Ok, I'm having a moment.

One of those, when doubts and questions come. I know they like to hang with me. I recognise them, wave hello and hope at some point, they will go.

Even if I didn't listen to them, I'd still feel them. I feel my neck, it is stiff.

Ping.

What was this? Oh nothing. Just a reminder.

I set up a month-worth of them. A wellbeing reminder for every hour.

For my clients, I made another version. Lighter on the schedule, heavier on the brand. The *real ease reminders.* Three times a day with a video for each desk exercise.

What a great idea! Everybody loves them, nobody uses them, a client told me.

I know it's true. That's how I use them too.

Ping, check, snooze.

Sometimes, when I feel conscious of my creation, when I remember my initial intention, when my partner looks in my direction,

I'd strike a pose. I'd breathe deeper. I'd stretch myself.

It feels nice, I know.

I wish I could short circuit judgement, simply act on my wellbeing resolution.

That's what I should do. Judge myself less, trust myself more. Especially if I want others to trust me.

I know it shows. The mental talk, the self-deception, the inner tension.

What if I could snooze my mental pings?

Maybe then, I would stop distracting myself. Maybe then, I would hear myself again.

Helper syndrome

I wanted to help people feel better and healthier at work, a beautiful thing indeed.

But there I was, entangled in my confusion.

Had I been able to step back, I would have recognised that I needed to be stable before I could give a hand.

Had I been there for myself first, I would have done healthier in my venture.

Puzzled, I was searching for pieces of identification in my action. Helpless, I couldn't see the bigger picture.

I was helping in the hope to get my attention.

The helper
who claims
itself
is a helpee
screaming
for help.

Shooting wellbeing en passant

I was helpless at feeling well.

Shooting wellbeing services at everyone. Sharing tips, reminders and awareness wherever I could.

Hoping the world would benefit from me as I kept wasting my energy.

Well, that's not fair to say, all my efforts didn't go astray.

Some bullets did hit me.

I guess I should thank myself then, for putting up such a wellbeing show.

No one to blame, only to entertain.

Expert syndrome

If you see me dance, you will see me jump ecstatically.

This is how much energy I have, when I use it well and canalised. When I don't, I hop on and off, from imposter to expert.

Those moments are easy to find to this day. Simply look at my LinkedIn page.

See the calls to action squeezed in branded self-exposure? See the tension between the lines, telling the story of forced authenticity?

See the inner cringe, showing on the lines of my face? As I attempt to articulate what I try to become.

A self-appointed wellbeing expert. The one you need, to feel better at work.

See the intensity of my social presence and inner absence?

See my name between the titles of honour, giving my self a reason to be worth?

Hold on, who put that music on?

Why should I call myself names? When being me means so much more, than expertise can ever give me.

What if
we were
the ones
who made
it all too
difficult?

Taking
what feels right

I don't care for best practices.

Not for success step-by-step, not for lead magnets. No matter how well documented. No matter how thorough.

I tried, I encountered my sabotage and rebellion at their best. I cursed myself.

If it works for others, it should work for me too. I am not stupid, I should be able to apply them, to follow through.

All I need, I thought, *is a little more discipline.* No big deal.

But it is. A deal against me.

Crippling self-talk takes over as I rebel.

The blame, the critic. They judge me guilty, ill-spotted lazy. They are the signs, these best ways aren't mine.

I owe it to myself, to my singularity, to my natural tendency. I owe it to my wellbeing, to be picky with what works for me.

Masseters at work

Now that I spent another morning outpowering my masseter,

now that tears ran down my cheeks without ruining my make-up,

now that I cursed myself for falling in that trap again: *what companies want to hear isn't what I want to say,*

maybe I can stop giving a damn and be fine, just being the petite dame I am.

Beliefs in a why

I started with a *why* that shone.

A *why* that shone too bright for my own good,

a *why* that kept me blind like sun rays on a wet pavement.

I kept walking.

why not?

Eyes closed, something would tell me when to stop.

Self in deception

Self-deception makes sense,
if you believe you have a self to preserve.

When you realise that you don't,
you can drop it.

Between farmers

A being in its element is an expert by nature.
So are seeds growing in the right field and
fashion.

Becoming an expert at anything that lies outside of me
for the sake of corporate credibility, is out of place, out of
strength and out of purpose.

Why attempt to feel grounded so far away from yourself?

If you feel off, if you feel overexposed and estranged, at the
very end of that field, you certainly are.

Don't plant yourself under pressure, don't seed whatever
others are seeking and selling.

Who cares, what crop is on demand?

Only you know, what kind of sprout you are.

When it is, you feel at peace and centred. Where it is, you shine your best light.

Whether you root deep or pierce through the ground.

Whether you do well in deserts or wetlands.

Whether you care to rise from the warmth or prefer to hang somewhere cooler.

When you respect your crop, you know where to grow.

Mother of talent

> Natural predispositions were revealed
> to me. Even those I wasn't fond of. Since
> I was committed to lead my life with my
> ego for a while, I dismissed their evidence.
> Only to look back and see them waiting in
> line as I wave at them.

She said it, *Oui maman,*[21] in response to the advice I'd given.
*If you are sick. Let yourself be sick. Give it to your body, that
ill-deserved rest.*

There it was again, the mummy stamp.

I am everybody's mum. A mum for adults, that is.

The one who sees how well you do from afar.

The one who stands there for you, still as a mirror.

The one who listens and repeats, so you may hear yourself.

The one who feeds you back, with your own thoughts, gestures, and behaviours.

With *Oui maman,* I saw it. My predisposition held her position all these years.

It was the same, when my brother claimed the obvious, he didn't need a second mother.

When schoolfriends confessed to me, I was called the *faculty mum.*

When I assisted my cat in labour. As sweet as she was, she never missed a booty call from nature.

Yes, lady mother of all kinds, I still didn't want to be one.

Meet your experts

You wouldn't be who you are without the voices in your head. The ones that are yours.

I identified three of mine. The wellbeing voice, the thinker and the writer. They were my company as I wrote this book.

Sometimes we had fun together. Often, I would ask them questions. Each time, I would roll my eyeballs.

They always had an answer.

I am sure you can find yours up there. If you pay attention.

> Don't be appalled by the noise.
> These voices are your experts.
> Each of them telling you where to look,
> to come closer to yourself. All of them,
> in their apparent complexity, reminding
> you how simple *being you* can be.

Don't look for ranking in their credibility or legitimacy.

They all have a right exist, to express themselves accordingly.

Be mindful of your inner peers, let them be heard.

Forget about judging and censoring, engage with them.

It is in this vibrant diversity, that you can give way to who you are. Relying on your being, you are less tempted to chase experts outside yourself.

Those, no matter how much sense they make to your senses, will never speak up for yourself, as well as you can.

Quoted
à mes côtés[22]

I like to cite you.

Yes, you *by my side*. You in my network.

It's with you I share my experience, not with someone whose name and words are famous.

You and me, we met. We sparked, we enlightened each other.

We moved our worlds in and out, just as we moved each other.

I choose not to chase or praise. No one higher, no one bigger.

A big name is no real deal, not more than you and me.

If we want to flatten hierarchies,

if we want equal chances in a fairer society,

why not start with our words?

I won't look much further than you. I won't ask you to work

harder and faster. I won't need you to better and stronger.

Let's be where we are.

Together with our people, our peers, our friends. Those directly around us, those we can inspire.

It is by choosing to credit those we can reach, by recognising those we can look in the eyes, by sharing expertise with those we can experience,

that we can fully be and grow together.

So, call in your people today. Give them the praise and thanks they deserve, for being a present with you.

IN LINE

Searching for a living

I long felt I was failing at being legitimate.

I rebelled against researching facts and figures. I fell asleep while reading studies. I disconnected before the abstract ended.

Why stop so soon? Why cut myself short before the concrete stuff has begun?

Simply, I wasn't looking for this.

The credibility I searched had to come from within.

Just like you are, I am my own research.

I am empirical in my experience.

A living proof in my own terms.

A truth where being one, is more than enough.

If expertise
builds on the
full experience
– from its
absence to its
presence –
we all qualify
as wellbeing
experts.

IN LINE

Knowing does not bite

That's a good and peaceful thing indeed.
Since no one,
when master of their own world,
needs to compete with another.

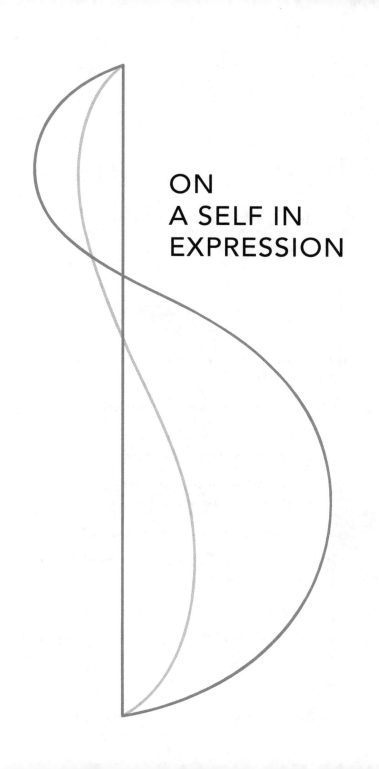

ON
A SELF IN
EXPRESSION

There's a woman on you, lady

I knew I came for a beating. Still, that heel there in my liver, is not what I pictured.

I never felt it before. Now I can. My persecuted organ feels big, the size of a fist.

The more she pushes against it, the harder it gets. Like ball of anger ready to fire.

The supressed emotion tries an escape.

Confused, my liver bubbles up. That's how trauma vents, running through the abdomen.

After years of hanging inside, it's now looking for a way out.

The alert reaches the neighbours. My organic aches seek asylum and find refuge in my chest. I suffocate.

Breathe deeper, says my friend and therapist.

She did warn me, *working emotions out of the body is like*

dancing with a lumberjack. While Sandy dances gracefully on me, I am her dancefloor.

No air comes out. How can I breathe? *Open your mouth more.*

I need to fake it, take whatever my lungs will give me.

There it is. My voice leaves a stream of weak air.

A whisper for help.

This is how bodies speak while they process their inner hell.

Here comes a cough. Erratic. Deep. Nowhere near my control.

My body trembles, I smile in victory. We got rid of a load. One of many more to follow.

Organ crashing

Emotions are language. When they aren't expressed, they find a place where they will wait. In the cushy couches of your organs. Until the overlooked is overbooked.

Your organs
were made
for working
properly,
not for
hosting your
emotional
Airbnb.

Piercing the clouds

If you go for anger, you are up for roller-coaster.

Unexpressed, it builds jaw-dropping mountains, with spikes of resentment.

Peaks that culminate so high, they pierce the fluffy clouds between subconscious and conscious.

They don't announce themselves as such. They prefer to show up in disguise through physical signs.

Tennis elbow, arthritis, stomach ulcers. All kinds of imaginative symptoms for the repressed emotions.[23]

Yes, nature made you more creative and expressive than you thought. And a tad over the top.

Wisdom in a bucket

Most of what I experienced is not worth placing on a list, even those involving a bucket. Not the most glamorous thing to say, but surely handy to hold on.

Anger tastes bitter

If I were born in the Middle Ages with my red hair, I wouldn't have lasted long before being consumed on a bonfire.

Still, there I was with another witch, burning myself with a stick and with my consent.

It was my third kambo,[24] I knew what came next in the process: the discomfort, the relief, the resulting frog-poison-facial-lift.

In between sessions, I dared to show my puffy cheeks at a startup event. I travelled from Luzern where the burning took place to Zurich to breathe and stretch with entrepreneurs. Despite my swollen face, I could still articulate.

Back to the pit, in a room smudged with sage, my bucket was waiting for me.

Before I'd let anything out, I had to take more in.

The upcoming purge was not the worst thing. While my

turbulent waters were fighting to come up, I still had one more litre to get down.

My shamanic host applied frog venom on my skin, to the burnt dots covering my back, arms and stomach.

She poured more water and left me alone.

The drumming and chanting started again as I struggled for each nauseous breath. An intense heat wave came from within, followed instantly by shivering.

With a strength I ignored, my hands gripped the plastic container and wouldn't let go for half an hour.

Emotions don't invade us to leave without a trace the next day. When we throw a party, we – the hosts – have to clean up.

Beer cans, half empty glasses, guacamole turning brown and crisps greasing the floor.

These are the leftovers going bad, our hormonal baggage getting old, our protein cocktails moulding on our organic walls. Emotional party after party.

My parties were thrown in the liver, full of unprocessed anger and belittled frustrations. They gathered in puddles of rage and resentment.

Waiting for the day I'd wash them away.

Draft on pressure

> There is a term in writing called *vomit draft*. It refers to the first phase of self-expression. The first jet of thoughts and words as they escape the mental space and collide with a blank page.

Because it is raw and barely digested by reason, it is ugly to look at. Some claim this is art.

With my phobia of vomiting, I wasn't ready.

With shamanic medicine, I learnt to face what I had hidden inside.

This is how I started to write.

Revolt for action

Revolting emotions trigger my observation and my need for expression.

This, I inherited from my father. He could have excelled as a lawyer or writer.

He wasn't any of that, still he addressed letters of justice to whomever he judged deserved one.

On and off, calls for expression would come and disturb my poise. I'd take a keyboard and type on.

Whether I liked its tone or not, my revolt had the right to come out. I used it to write, I gave it a shape, in a melodic pamphlet.

Go ahead, meet my ruffled bears! Welcome them for what they are, an invitation for self-expression.

Let them ping our shortcomings. Let them make us think, take us on a ride within.

This is how we ensure that what's unfair,

won't be left unattended out there.

Creating worlds with words

The thoughts I thought shattered the ones I created before.

Sometimes they'd match. Often they'd mix.

You can think all you want about me, as you read these pages.

I may be a maniac, I may be a narcissist. Maybe I go border-line with my personality, with an exceeding attention to my deficit.

Does this qualify as a disorder or is this just a trait, a character?

Wait, this is no trait, she calls that a wellbeing line.

Traits or lines, I may be missing squares up there. I may have too many boxes I will never tick. Not even on productive days.

What is she thinking now?

Well, it's simple. Everything and its opposite.

I believe this applies to most of us. The ones who dare to say, the ones who feel they know.

Even if knowing starts where credibility stops. In the eyes of society. In the eyes of our sanity.

Who cares about credibility when there is certainty?

We feel more than we can tell.

We are more than life can conceive.

We live more than rules can regulate.

We don't need to function.

We don't need to be cared for.

We don't need to belong.

We exist, all ready as we are.

As the living proof that the social, the personal, the professional li(v)es we've built around ourselves, don't need us to work for them any longer,

if they don't work for us anymore.

Clearing mental pipes

This morning I washed my hair.

I know, great start!

The water in the bathroom has been running slow.

When it drains well, the bathtub pipe gurgles happily. This morning, it didn't.

Looking at my red hair streaming down the pipe, I realised there was nothing there. Nothing to prevent the block.

As I sat down by the window with a third cup of tea, I remembered how I explained energy clearing to a friend the day before. Between hair clogs in water pipes and judgements, there was no difference. When we keep playing those stale old thoughts to ourselves, we're up for a block.

This morning, I reckoned it was my responsibility to let things flow freely.

For my bathtub, I wouldn't give it a second thought. I would remove the block with salt, baking soda, add some warmed-up vinegar.[25] Others would use chemical products or force, and pump it all up.

But why keep using products or therapy, to remove what blocks me? Why not use a filter as a preventive measure? Choosing instead consciously, what I allow to run through me?

Contradictions better out than in

Why apologise for contradictions?

As I sit in the only plantless room of the house, I play a list called *music for plants*.

Some of my contradictions are more profound. So deep, that no one outside myself ever gets a glance to judge them.

The only judge there is then, must be me.

Expressing further

Yes right here, right now.

What are the words that make you cringe? What are the battles you fight within?

If you catch yourself, forcing more than flowing, faking more than enjoying. You are stretching yourself far and thin.

Write them all down, the words which bother you. The ones you feel are working against you.

Be open with yourself. Have no fear, no judgement.

What else would you feel, if you didn't try to hide or suppress anything?

Which words would you choose to tell about yourself, if you were the only one to read them?

Take one, and cut

> I started writing when I was doubting everything about myself and my wellbeing business. Desperate to find myself stuck again, I had to vent. In a timid voice on a mountain top, I told my partner *I just want to write.*

I promised, this time, I wouldn't pretend I was doing fine, running myself mad with my *busyness* around.

I wouldn't stay hyperactive in town. Maybe I should move to the countryside.

My overachiever still in charge, two meetings with my professional crowd were enough to put my resolve aside.

I got myself a return ticket for the ego trip I was trying to offboard. I decided to write with a purpose and a plan.

My book would be grant, a perfect business card! The book of a wellbeing expert for entrepreneurs and corporate drop-outs.

In the process, I repeated my patterns. I told myself more stories:

the highs and lows of a specialist in corporate wellbeing, the tale of a solopreneur who never stopped struggling, the wisdom of a woman who trusted that in the end, she'd reach success and fame.

I kept myself in the business loop, I kept my self at bay a little further.

I followed more trainings online, I reinvented myself as a coach for professionals.

I signed an expensive rental contract, I opened a wellbeing practice in my own flat.

I reflected on money when it came to me easily, I wondered why then, it decided to leave me.

With nothing more to run after than the image I created, I had to distance myself again.

I started to take myself out of the way.

I planted my feet in the ground, I went for walks in nature, any time of the day.

I played with time and creativity. I ditched outlines that no longer fitted me.

I decided to live more simply. As a woman who respected herself for who she was already.

Slowly, I understood that writing had little to do with my business, I had little tips to give for wellbeing success.

The book I was writing had nowhere new to take me.

It was a world of words as sharp as mirrors, so I could cut the crap while I was living it.

Femme affamée

Fame[26] is hunger, always chasing after, running after something that hasn't been given.

The missing attention of a parent.

The lacking validation of a corporation,

The forbidden emotion of a self in expression.

Feeling express

How many trains of thought have you missed to express?

How many emotions have you kept unspoken and suppressed?

How many tensions have you encountered and left to linger?

> Your ability to attend to what you feel is real. So why wait, to treat yourself with awe and respect? Recognise the swift impulses of your being, right there and when they appear.

Learn to speak the language of your being, beneath the streams of passing thoughts and emotions. Be they positive or negative, be they uplifting or downgrading. Don't judge them.

They came your way for a reason that your reason may not understand. They came to be seen, beyond what they seem to be. They came for something only your self can:

expression, integration, transformation.

With time and repetition, you'll get accustomed to the process. You'll notice that *being* has little to *do* with them.

Behind the noise and the agitation, beyond the scattered attention and calls for action, all you are left with is yourself. With a being and a feeling.

And perhaps then, you'll remember what all this time, you couldn't explain.

You'll remember what you've known, ever since you felt.

Intuitively, without second guessing. Without proving nor justifying.

You've known it with intimate certainty, in every corner of your being.

You've known that feeling is knowing.

Expression of the moment

If we were to wait for that moment,

until we feel strong and certain,

until we are sure and confident, from all the information we could ever gather,

we would only speak once.

Once and too late.

An atrocious bunch of contradictions. Inaudible and unbearable.

For the listener and for yourself.

After this once-in-a-lifetime iteration, we would be ready to call it a night. A night forever.

So, express yourself, every single day. Through your profession, through your passion, through your sensation, through your action and your inaction, through your self.

For yourself and for others.

No one should expect you to be perfect.

No one should ask you to know it all.

No one should value the opinion of an expert and dismiss the expression of a stranger.

We shall all consider ourselves, experts of the moment. All incredible and credible as we are. All infamous artists of our being. All perfectly able to create, a life full of impermanent imperfection. Because who we were today, what we said already, no longer exists.

What I write
today is true
today.
What I realise
tomorrow
will be written
tomorrow.

Emotions need you to be

There are emotions we are fond of. They feel nice, warm and fuzzy. Others we don't like so much. We shame ourselves for them.

They are not cool. Not acceptable in the eyes of others. Not good enough to uplift our ego either.

They are a disgrace to the image we've worked so hard to paint of our selves. All these extra hours, all this time spent working and networking to earn something worth telling.

I used to think that way. Now I feel more.

> I don't see positive and negative emotions. I see creative motion, prone to doing and living. I see therapeutic expression, not to be suppressed under pretence of inadequacy.

Your emotional wellbeing isn't to be ignored.

It is here to be explored.

Be the change
I want to see

I took an afternoon break from writing and reached for a book to switch gears. I bought it off a coffee shop thanks to a note on the shelf. It said it could be mine for ten swiss francs and the title promised I would understand my feminine brain.

Eventually I did. Through practice, not through reading.

I opened the book to the first page.

Instinctively I flipped further.

Three minutes later, I stopped. I wanted to change the ways in which life was written.

Why couldn't I fake patience? Why couldn't I start on page one and read steadily?

I want to jump to the point, to the one I desire.

Time doesn't need to matter, I don't want it to.

> There is no straight line, no obligation for linear consumption. Not in my life, nor in this book.

Realisations can take me by surprise, I have the space to catch them.

So, jump to whatever catches your eye.

Seize what you are ready to see.

Browse, go through, take shortcuts, let timing come to you.

When your mind is free, your heart is open to receive your self with it.

Revealing the process

I gave space in this book to my repetitive, sometimes overindulging observations.

I chose to let them be there, I had to let myself be as well.

Not because I had a great message. Not because I felt good about what I had to tell.

Reflections were the rock of my mental and emotional wellbeing as I ventured in my wellbeing exploration through self-expression.

To me, they depicted a universal struggle, a need for self-justification, as we take the courage to expose our innermost critic.

Ourselves.

At least, the one we think we are, until we let it express itself.

Making space for the new

As I opened my manuscript to write a new entry, scrolling down to find a space for new words between the old,

I held myself back. No stepping forward, not even in another direction.

I kept myself in the air, not knowing where to land.

Fingers on halt. Nothing left to type.

Aware of what happened, I'll open a blank page next time. There I'll find space to move.

There I'll start something new.

Editing conversation

66 *For the first two thirds of it, I didn't know why I was reading it.*

Fair enough.

This is how I went about my wellbeing business.

This is how I went about living life.

66 *Don't give the impression that you are overindulging in what you write.*

Well, that's a bummer.

Me, who wanted to lead by example.

To tell you that precisely,

it's ok to be that way,

whatever way that is.

Feedback from yourself

As I sent out an excerpt of my manuscript for feedback, I knew what I would receive.

What I could think of my work is what I got back.

The good like the bad.

Some would seize the sparks between the lines. Others would wave at my inner wobble.

In exposing my being and shortcomings, I put my personal leadership in application.

I could see how we mirror each other.

Don't believe me. Experiment for yourself.

Express whatever it is you have inside. Be ready to feel and create, be open to receive and recognise.

There they are, your thoughts, handed back to you.

Anything
I got myself
to think, I got
it. Provided,
I was the one
who thought
for it.

Letting it exist

There are countless ways to express yourself. The ones that are accepted by your peers may not be the right ones for you.

Find your own way and take your time, take detours if you care.

No one can tell you what to say, unless you let them.

> If you gave me this book a year ago so that I may write today, I would have called you names. Any name for that matter, as long as it weren't mine.

Being
in writing

My word editor tells me I'm doing it wrong. It prompts me to change *"be* your best" to *"do* your best".

But I mean what I say, I want you to *"be* yourself", not to *"do* yourself".

Even if doing is enjoyable and colloquial... Wouldn't we be in a better place,

if the language we used every day helped us with *being* as much as *doing*?

Life would
not let me
rest. Until I
accepted that
being myself,
was all
I had to do.

IN LINE

Welcome content

I'd like you to welcome an unapologetic version of yourself.

Because your wellbeing depends on it.

Welcome your aches, your moods, your temper.

Welcome your need for structure and its aversion.

Welcome your love for freedom and a longing for something stable.

Welcome everything you think you are and its opposition.

Welcome your complexity in all simplicity.

Since this book is a mirror, read again these welcoming lines, replacing yours with mine.

I ask you to allow contradictions, in you as much as in me.

For as long as we consider ourselves separate, to allow others is to allow your self.

Witnessing the writing

I met an author at a conference. She asked me how my book was doing. *It is writing itself,* I answered.

It was accurate. I made a pact with myself: the book would tell me what it wants to say as we'd go through the process.

I would lend my hands and brain, a golden pen and paper, a MacBook and something called reMarkable. I wouldn't stand in its way.

How I write is beyond myself. Not to suit any standards, not to crawl under expectations.

I observe guidelines to dismiss them when I turn my back. I set deadlines, to then edit as long as it longs for.

And while we're here, we're still at it.

IN LINE

Words as mirrors

My words are here to make you think. They are the mirrors I have encountered, the mirrors I have hung up for myself, so I could stop walking blindly.

Your understanding will be different.

And this matters.

How are your words inspiring you? How would you define them based on your own and unique experience of the world, in and around your self?

Subjectivity, when expressed outside egotistic agendas, becomes welcome, for its collective truth.

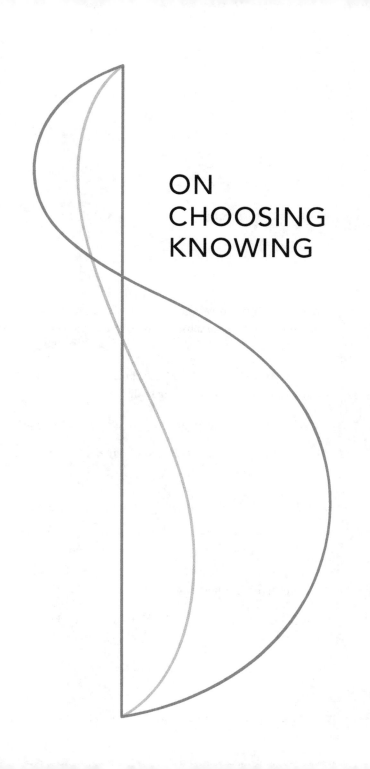

ON
CHOOSING
KNOWING

Based on what you liked

What if the overdose of choices made us insensible to ourselves? Numb to the sense of who we are. Stranger to who we want to be.

If the *you* you've been, is the sum of the choices you've made against yourself, you're not going to like what you see.

Ask yourself, honestly, would you go to see a movie blindly?

Yes, you can indulge in not choosing. You can follow others' recommendations a little longer.

> Netflix is not the only place where you cruise more than you choose, based on where you've been before.

But is this how you shall live?

Binge-living on a series of trends and feeds fed by your neighbours?

Just for a change

Consumption isn't mandatory.
Because we're saturated with it and
being used for it, doesn't mean we
have to encourage it.

Each to their own

To become who we are, we project our life lessons on everything outside ourselves.

The actor is the director. The student is the teacher.

We plot our stories, we direct and produce them, with or without money.

We screen them on the walls of sleep at night, to write our critique the next day.

We sell our rights, we sell ourselves short, hoping that's what others will buy.

Why should they bother watching us? Aren't they too busy making up their own movie?

Dietary question

Your breastfeeding years have long been over.

It is time you feed yourself consciously, time you question accordingly.

What is it, that makes who you are?

What is it, you're buying into?

Which nutrition, whose information, what mode of consumption?

What are you choosing today, to build your self upon?

Feed yourself accordingly

> You won't settle for compote if you crave tuna. It's a clear fact, no matter how it's looked at. You can't deceive yourself like that.

5 pm, dinner time. In the pantry, as minimalist as my flat: pear compote; tomato sauce; courgettes; pre-cooked beet-root; mustard; turnips; canned tuna and ground hazelnut.

As I feel the urge to write but won't let expression run, I distract myself with supper. My brain relaxes whenever I mix spices and chew on nuts. Quieting the censors at the gates of ideation, leaving me with a spoon in my mouth and a plate on my lap, when I wish I had a pen in my hand.

My instinct jumps to fish, my inner controller disagrees.

No you can't have that, why open a tin tonight? Save it for another day and settle for something else.

I open each door again. Cupboard, fridge, pantry. Pantry, fridge, cupboard. Oh yes, fresh blueberries!

I take an empty jar and proceed in layers. Pear compote, blueberries, hazelnut. Sit on the balcony, eat it all and reflect on the last chunk.

I know, mindful eating.

My body still misses something. A tart taste and the promised proteins. I won't fight.

Go, make me another one!

A bed of tuna, a sprinkle of mustard seeds, a big splash of garlic mayo. There you go.

By the time I sit down again, I know what I've done to myself. By refusing the clear call for tuna, I shoved something else instead and so much more in the end.

Tuna was art. Mustard seeds, my prose and observations. Garlic mayo, my wellbeing products and videos. Teaching yoga, for berries. Running a business, for the nuts.

And my advertising career in all that? A sweet base of pear compote, with a homemade sticker on top.

Going om

Anywhere I look, I see the reflection of my limitations.

Wherever I stand, I am surrounded by walls I wish I could break free from.

No matter what I say, it's for the sake of my own thoughts and actions.

My social wellbeing line has gone loose. I know it, I feel it.

This is what losing myself feels like.

Dull and heavy.

I can't go on, meeting with you if I'm not inspired, walking through this office if I'm not exalted.

Nothing needs to last longer, once I realise it isn't mine.

> Take good note of your wellbeing signals.
> Erratically mental, dramatically emotional,
> shamingly financial, brutally physical.
> Wellbeing doesn't discriminate.

So hold on tight, there is no chance to dismiss them.

Take a last look around, grateful for the time you spent with them.

And move on.

There is no shame in walking home on your own.

I'm not sure where we are, but we're in this together.

Lunita

My aunt once said I was lunatic.
That's right, I am a resident of the earth,
a neighbour of the moon.

If I can live with neighbours, I can live
with that.

Socially fond of me

What happens to you?

When you decide to hang out a bit more your own and lonely self.

Don't you ever do that?

Because it's too boring. Because you fear who awaits you there.

How can you wish for fulfilling relations, for fruitful collaborations?

When you always run away. When you keep finding excuses for not seeing yourself.

But how would your world be?

If only we started by dating ourselves.

If we were deeply in love, vulnerable and honest, with our own quiet mess.

Isn't it pretentious of us to pretend, we care about feeling well, when we don't even feel ourselves?

Projection on the map

You are here.

I wish I were, a red dot on my map.

One I could use to navigate my inner world. One to show me the right places, to take me out of the wrong situations.

Not that there is a right or wrong per se. All locations and situations can reveal themselves as beneficial. Still, they don't need to be mine.

Ever since I felt myself, I know I should have known,

my feeling is my knowing.

It is my red dot, whether I spot it or not.

Before I blink my eyes open, the room is bathed with the colours of my next decisions.

My inner certainty is beamed, blunt and bright for me to see, long before you interact with me.

When I fail to see what I know, I spread my delusion on you. And this is all I'll get back from you.

How confusing, I could blame you for that! But why would I?

You just painted a scene with me, with the emotional colours I gave you. You mixed them up, stretched them into thin lines, spotted me right there in the middle, in my disgracious dot.

There, indeed, I am.

With the depicted picture of my feelings and decisions, further developed in our relation.

Ranking myself in the charts

My questions were simple. Where did I come from, when I took my first breath? What subtle-ware did I come with, when I landed in the open space?

I'd skim through books, look for answers in tea and pie charts. Ask anyone, from shamans to strangers on a seaside. Gaze at maps, hang in messy places.

I'd find fun facts, entertain theories and fantasies. An equal part of talent and doubt to be traced back to Chiron in my chart. An aura that intimidates and attracts, thanks to Lilith, the moon in black.

In a quiet space at my centre, I'd find certitude. From where I stood, there would be no one like me.

No one to tell me, what my life should be. No one to say, where my next step would lead.

To remember who I was, I wouldn't have to look far out. From my perspective, I would remain, my one and only.

Playing life with yourself

This life game you play is yours. Because playing is a serious thing, you've set yourself to forget what you were doing.

Like a five-year-old, you opened your present, got hyped at your new toy and dismissed the instruction manual.

And guess who cleaned after you?

Society – if I were to blame the system.

Your parents – if I were to ask a therapist.

You – if I were to awaken spirituality.

But who knows really? Could have been my great aunt Gaby. She liked to throw our stuff away, to keep the house tidy. When asked if she saw what I was searching, she'd wave her empty hands.

Me? I haven't touched anything!

Why search for rules and instructions? Had you read them, you would have refused to play.

What if we didn't have to play games against ourselves?

Worm wisdom

Fruits from your garden are the real thing, the real you. They contain your essence and flavour, your inhabitants compatible by nature.

As I sliced a pear open for my afternoon break, I met one of its tenants. A worm whirling inside, carving its way through the centre.

The closer I cut to the worm's habitat, the stiffer the flesh. I removed the rooms it once occupied and kept the rest to eat it intact.

Since the pear was given to me with a red apple, I went on with my exploration. Preparing fruits for consumption, I later gathered, was as beneficial as self-exploration.

When you take time to look inside, with a calm and curious mind, you prepare yourself to face the fauna of your flora.

There, you meet your stiffening beliefs and self-consuming

judgments, your biased doubts and crippling fears. All of them live under your surface. They feed off your resources.

When you are aware you may see them there, you can deal with them more consciously.

You can choose not to identify with the thoughts and the stories you see. You can decide whether to define yourself through them. Whatever their origin, whatever their nature.

Had I faced my wormy insides on a first date, I would have thrown myself away. A shout in disgust, a flying knife across the table, a true waste of potential.

A traumatic encounter indeed, abrupt and dramatic. The opposite of romantic.

Yet my authentic self, the tastier version of myself, comes in its natural form. Like these pear and apple.

As I sat on the floor with edible pieces in my hand, I knew how lucky I was.

These tiny fruit parts, as raw as I was, were the best ones I ever had.

Working your feeling muscle

No matter our subjective nature. We remain equal.

Equal in our capacity to feel ourselves, as we go about our individual lives.

No matter how hard we think, we all have a powerful muscle in common. A feeling muscle. It connects to our wellbeing state, at the base of our being.

I call it feeling muscle because there is a real, tangible physical sensation to wellbeing.

It is the delicious, the soothing and heart-warming, the comforting experience we feel, when we trust ourselves.

When joy sparks with certainty.

When we remember that all is well, we know that everything we cannot understand, indeed makes sense.

Call it intuition, call it meditation.

Call it heart space, call it alpha brainwave.

Call it whatever you want.

Explain it in scientific terms, believe it from the spiritual realm.

The name, the description, the application of this feeling, is not what wellbeing is about.

What being is about, is your experience of it.

Wellbeing
is knowing
you can trust
yourself,
beyond
what you
understand.

Feel better lighter

Feeling is a reliable way to decipher options, to move in line and forward, staying light and nimble in your heart.

Use it in your life, in your love. In your profession, in your vocation.

Feeling is not about sensing emotions. Feeling is a pure and fine sensation.

Whatever feels heavy, whatever constricts, drives you to the opposite direction.

So don't force and fool yourself, don't carry weights and stories around.

Don't drag and drop yourself through life.

Or try if you want. It will hit you back with lessons that aren't made in cotton.

Subscribe to your channel

I am on Skype with my channeler, his name is Michael, like the archangel. I hired the latter to cut shiny blue ropes for me.

This Michael here, is my projector. He tells me words of wisdom, scribbles them on a piece of paper, so I can see, drawn clearly, what truth is dormant inside me.

I *know* what he tells me. It feels right, hence it is true.

It resonates in my skull, it hums in my chest.

I don't need to back up what he says. I don't need to look for data to soothe my reason, search for proofs or means of comparison.

I know it from my deepest sensation, there is nothing more valid to me, than what I feel now.

In this moment, in my position.

I am the data.

I am more research than I will ever put together. I am the subject at the centre of all objective endeavour.

The one who gives all meaning, to the life I am living.

Why would
I ever doubt?
There's no
clearer truth
to me than
the one I
broadcast.

Running out but wiser

If everyone was searching for enlightenment, my yoga teacher said, *the world would run out of business.*

I don't think it would.

And while we're here,

I don't think we need to search anything.

So, how about we just keep on being? Simply living, a little wiser. Starting today.

> 66 *... the planet does not need more successful people. But it does desperately need more peacemakers, healers, restorers, storytellers, and lovers of every kind. It needs people who live well in their places. It needs people of moral courage willing to join the fight to make the world habitable and humane. And these qualities have little to do with success as we have defined it.*
>
> *David W. Orr*[27]

I knew
I could choose

I stand on the sofa, because I can. I know she is coming to see me again.

The lights beam from the kitchen door. Grandparents and great aunts sit at the breakfast table.

I hear the cling song of the spoons whirling in bowls of milk coffee. Although I'm not at the table, I can see them. Aunt Marceline eats the crust of her tartine now spongy, she fishes the pieces one by one from her morning brew. My mother is sitting there too.

She left me with my brother on the sofa, as we emerge from our sleep in a comforting darkness. She never switched on the lights for us, she wouldn't interfered with our waking process.

She carried us down from dreaming to living, wrapped in a blanket. With each crack of the wooden stairs, I marvelled at my mother's strength and care.

She is right, to let us simmer in our grogginess a little longer. At this time of the day, we don't play, we don't fight yet. There's no need for competition, not for her love, not for attention.

Ever since I've been, my brother has been there with me. Snuggling under the nightgown of another Auntie, thick like a duvet, with buttons covered in fabric. He holds them between his fingers. One can go loose, she won't be upset.

Like kittens paw at their mother's breast, I'm waiting for mine. I pound the sofa with my feet, I'm done with the rest.

My first decision of the day. She turns on the light. I'm ready to go first.

She pulls out clothes from the cherry wood wardrobe and holds them up for me to see. I keep rocking softly from side to side, pulling my knees even higher.

There goes to my morning workout, before I even thought I needed one. Movement activates my brain, my tummy tells me what I like from what I don't. My ego in development is in ecstasy.

Here I am, I get to choose!

At least, most of the time. Some days, my favourite pieces get stuck in traffic, between washing and ironing. I then receive the *short-culotte*[28] with its white woollen socks. I welcome them with unconditional fury and resentment.

Don't tell me what to wear. Don't tell me what to look like.

Not a minute spent in a *short-culotte* day, will help me feel another way.

When I decide based on what I feel, I win the lottery.

I could win every day of my life. With the conniving smile of my mother to boost my stubborn assertion, I know how right I am.

Today's winner fits me like a glove. It is a soft sweatshirt starring the same house and the same cat, always. It observes the outside world through the window. Ready for another day, happy and undisturbed from where it stands.

As a child
I knew

I knew it as a child, I had to learn it again.

After years of socialisation.

After years of trying, pretending and failing.

After feelings of unwell, and the responsibility for perpetrating them.

The time I spent, simply being and reflecting,
is the best thing I can do to myself.

Trading empathy for compassion

Say you meditate.

Say you don't, or not today. Say you're resting quietly and breathing deeply.

You hear the rain outside. It purrs and pours. Cat and cow, cats and dogs.

Right there, you feel a twitch in your heart. You inquire and go inside.

It is your bicycle. Loyal and handy. Wet and cold.

With its bare saddle who gave you comfort and support on your rides outside.

Inside you are. In the cosy warmth of your house. Mindfully drifting to your soaking companion, you feel sorry. Almost guilty. Conscious of your sensitive thought.

Can you let it be there? Can you let the damp and cold where they are? Can you stop feeling sorry and send them warmth instead?

There, you don't need to be where you aren't. You choose to trade empathy for compassion.

Everything
we do,
everything
we see,
everything
we feel,
is a choice.
In real or
in disguise.

Using the feeling

You know the wellbeing feeling.

You've experienced it more than once.

It is spacious in your chest. Warm or cool, if this is what you like best.

It is a great, soothing sensation. Fuzzy and calm, all at once.

This is what being you feels like. Living like no one else but yourself.

So, remember who you are being, feel the wellbeing feeling.

Use this sensation, this built-in compass in any life situation. Use it over and over again.

The more you feel it, the better you know yourself.

IN LINE

Being in doing

What if, besides being and feeling well, I want to keep on doing?

I am free to welcome the whole range of emotions,

I am creative to express a variety of opinions,

I am present to observe myself in any given situation,

I am gifted to work on what sparks my inspiration,

I am being and conscious.

Knowing that beyond what I feel, being beyond everything I know, I can do how I choose to.

Knowing how right you are

Everyone is unique and different. You, even more so.

Because you are you, you'll always be better for yourself than anyone else.

Of course, it sounds egotistic. What doesn't?

From where you stand, you're the only one experiencing this life.

This makes you the most qualified specialist in the wellbeing art of being yourself.

Complete in feeling

Feeling is always with you. Just as your body is.

Any thought you have can be felt. Any action happens in and around the boundaries of your body.

Anything you perceive through your physical senses flows through you in a hormonal torrent. It binds itself through words and emotions, it travels to your heart and makes itself a reason.

I know, these categories – the physical, the mental, the emotional, the social, the financial – aren't easy to handle.

Or wait, maybe they are. If we stop handling them as separate.

Let them all melt in your *being*, in that mighty all-knowing you, since it can feel everything.

Now that we think the same about feeling, we can move on and know ourselves without boundaries.

Where on pacha was I?

My eyes are closed. I think they are.

I blink consciously, I can't tell the difference.

It starts again, I get ready. Sit a little straighter on the floor, hold my knees and rock back and forth. I breathe deeper.

I'm not giving birth, though it's some kind of labour. Hours of silent weeping already, I'm still in the midst of it.

The urge to shout comes from the bottom of my spine, my abdomen contracts.

If I could feel my body, I bet it would hurt. But my mind protects me, it took out the plug.

My chest collapses, I open my mouth. I let a soundless shout, I yell it all out.

Nothing in my control.

My eyes shut, I see them clearly. The light droplets floating away from me. Out of my body, into the void. They travel to a luxuriant forest, they become part of the picture. Trees, animals, flowers, mountains. There goes my pain, my sadness finds shelter.

This was my intention. I asked medicine to help me release the fear I carried. This feeling I had, this fear was never mine. Yet I was dragging it around, it kept dragging me down. For the petite lady I was, this was too much. I wanted to feel lighter, to live a little merrier.

The round is over my host says. It's *Pachamama,*[29] she covers me with her blanket of warmth and timeless love.

I lean back on a pillow. *Stay hydrated, dear.* I nod, she knows. How did my mouth get so dry? I used thousands of light droplets, litres of tears to paint scenes of soothed sorrow. *Agüita de la vida*[30] brings me in awe for its beauty, she washes away the sadness there is to me.

In a skilled distraction, she puts on a light show, let me marvel at colours while I bear the process.

A thoughtful hand reaches for a bottle. Another hand removes the lid, so I drink. *How kind of her. She cared and carried me, since I was born.*

I talk about this young woman there. She lays in Peruvian mountains, miles away from her home.

Who is she?

Elodie, a voice tells me.

My face lights up. A name like a humming melody, I want to thank her parents for this honour, for letting me use her body.

I want to greet her. I reach for her hand with another at my disposal, shake it slowly. What soft skin she has!

Let me touch her face. Even softer!

Let me touch her hair. What a colour!

How lucky I am to *be,* here with her. How lucky we are, for who she is. If only she knew.

She giggles and rolls on the floor. There we can rest assured, she remembers.

IN LINE

What were you doing here?

As far as you are concerned, only you knew.

This book, this life, this purpose, this venture of yours, is all about you.

Even though you tried to play it cool, to apply the humble rules you learned in school.

Sooner than later, you have to be honest with yourself. You knew better than anybody else.

You knew who you were.

You knew what felt right.

You knew where to go.

You knew what you did and why.

I wrote this book to help you remember that.

I wrote it to remember my self.

You
is what this
is all about.

66 *I believe in the best in you. You believe in the best in me.*

My love and best mirror

Proud in postscript

In my favourite books, even in the best I've read, I could find a typo.

Gasping, I'd be upset at the editor.

On the next breath, I'd be proud of myself.

If I — Elodie, spotter of the *coquille coquine*[31] — could see this, then I too, shall leave a few for you.

Yes, I rejoice at this thought already, as you'll see the error and smile in victory!

Whatever we came here to find, my dear reader, whatever the deed indeed, we can be proud of who we are.

Acknowledgements

Maman, ma reine Elisabeth, pour ta beauté d'âme et ton bon sang de bon sens. Papa, pour avoir tant osé. Thomas, pour ton humour décalé et tes mots jamais mâchés. Mamie, pour ta présence, tout simplement.

Edu, for trusting me with everything you had inside, you've empowered me to do the same. Gabrielle and Roger, for your timeless loyalty and generosity. Gareth, for giving a title for this book we all love. Pete, Ali and Siman, for seeing the potential in the earliest lines. Ana, Francesca, Lisa, Ruzica, Sandra, Franzisca and Friederike from the Birdhaus Writers Group, for your consistent cheering, sharing and guidance. Francesca again, my dear friend, book designer and creative partner, you've been a blessing from the very beginning. My friends and former colleagues from the ad world, my ladies from Lean In Wellbeing, my fellow artists and entrepreneurs in Zurich and beyond, thank you for co-creating so many parts of this journey with me.

And you, my dear reader. Thank you for welcoming my words into your life, for trusting me with your mind and your heart.

Endnotes

1   Marianne Williamson is an American author, spiritual thought leader and activist. See Williamson, 1992.

2   This can be translated as *Oh my little Elodie, what's happening to you?*

3   David Carson is an American graphic designer, art director, and surfer. See MasterClass, 2021.

4   Mountain of the Swiss Plateau that offers a panoramic view over the city of Zurich.

5   Lyrics from *Sympathique,* a song by the American band Pink Martini which met a great success in France. See Pink Martini, 1997.

6   Acuity is an online scheduling tool acquired by Squarespace in April 2019. See Casalena, 2019.

7   *Krank* in German can be translated as *ill* or *sick.*

8   Julia Cameron is an American author of more than forty books, poet, novelist, songwriter, filmmaker, and playwright. See Cameron, 1992.

9   Davidson, 2020.

10 Michael J. Meade is an American author, mythologist and storyteller. See Sommer, 2021.

11 Burnout was recognised as an occupational phenomenon by the World Health Organization and included in the International Classification of Diseases (ICD-11) in May 2019. See World Health Organization, 2019.

12 See The Myers & Briggs Foundation and 16 Personalities for more information about the Myers-Briggs Type Indicator and the 16 Personality Types.

13 Kurt Tepperwein is a German entrepreneur, author and speaker on Mental Training and personal development topics.

14 Sommer, 2021.

15 *Dihei in Züri* in Swiss German can be translated as *at home in Zurich*.

16 "Lean In Circles are small groups of women who come together regularly to support each other." See LeanIn.org.

17 See Holmes, 2007.

18 *Badis* are public baths and designated swimming areas in lakes and rivers in Switzerland.

19 *Handy* and *Compi* are colloquial German words for *mobile phone* and *computer*.

20 Nusra Sahin is a Multidimensional Consciousness coach, author and speaker. See Sahin, 2020.

21 *Oui maman* can be translated as *yes mom*.

22 *À mes côtés* can be translated as *by my side.*

23 Dr. John E. Sarno was Professor of Rehabilitation Medicine at New York University School of Medicine, and best-selling author of several books establishing the psychosomatic nature of chronic pain. See Sarno, 2007.

24 "Kambo is a traditional ritual that uses the poison of the giant monkey frog, to purify the body and treat various health conditions." *See also* Eske, 2019.

25 Cleaning hack recipe from the Well+Good website. See Morton, 2018.

26 *Femme affamée* in French can be translated as *starving woman* and *Fame* in Italian as *hunger* or *starvation.*

27 David W. Orr is an American environmentalist, author and Paul Sears Distinguished Professor of Environmental Studies and Politics Emeritus. See Orr, 2005.

28 Loose-fitting shorts that look like skirts, also called *culottes* or *culotte shorts* in English.

29 *Pachamama* refers to *Mother Earth* in the Andean culture.

30 *Agüita de la vida* in Spanish can be translated as *water of life* and refers here to *ayahuasca*, a ceremonial psychoactive brew from the Amazon region used for spiritual and medicinal purposes. See also Leonard, 2020.

31 *Coquille coquine* in French can be translated as *mischievous typo.*

References

16 Personalities. "Nature: Thinking vs. Feeling." www.16personalities.com/articles/nature-thinking-vs-feeling. Retrieved January 2022.

Cameron, Julia. *The Artist's Way: A Spiritual Path to Higher Creativity.* New York: TarcherPerigee, 1992.

Casalena, Anthony. "Acuity Scheduling, the online appointment scheduling platform, joins Squarespace." Squarespace Newsroom, April 23, 2019. newsroom.squarespace.com/blog/acuity-scheduling-the-online-appointment-scheduling-platform-joins-squarespace. Retrieved January 2022.

Davidson, Katey. "What Are the Ayurveda Doshas? Vata, Kapha, and Pitta Explained." *healthline.* August 5, 2020. www.healthline.com/nutrition/vata-dosha-pitta-dosha-kapha-dosha#ayurveda-doshas. Retrieved January 2022.

Eske, Jamie. "Kambo: Can frog poison boost health?" *Medical News Today.* April 17, 2019. www.medicalnewstoday.com/articles/323689. Retrieved January 2022.

Holmes, Chet. *The Ultimate Sales Machine: Turbocharge Your Business with Relentless Focus on 12 Key Strategies.* Portfolio / Penguin Group, 2007.

LeanIn.org. "Lean In Circles." https://leanin.org/circles. Retrieved January 2022.

Leonard, Jayne. "What to know about ayahuasca." *Medical News Today.* January 31, 2020. www.medicalnewstoday.com/articles/ayahuasca. Retrieved January 2022.

Masterclass. "David Carson Teaches Graphic Design | Official Trailer | MasterClass." YouTube video, 2:15. April 22, 2021. www.youtube.com/watch?v=pJgvgD-vjIc. Retrieved January 2022.

Morton, Katie. "No Plumber, No Problem: Conquer Drain Clogs With These 4 Cleaners You Can Make From Pantry Staples." *Well+Good.* July 31, 2018. www.wellandgood.com/homemade-drain-cleaner/. Retrieved January 2022.

Orr, David W. in Stone, Michael. K and Barlow, Zenobia, eds. *Ecological Literacy: Educating Our Children for a Sustainable World.* San Francisco: Sierra Club Books, 2005.

Pink Martini. "Sympathique." Track 3 on *Sympathique.* Heinz Records, 1997. pinkmartini.com/discography/sympathique/. Retrieved January 2022.

Sahin, Nusra. *Multidimensional Consciousness And The New Earth: How To Master A Multidimensional Lifestyle.* Kindle Edition, 2020.

Sarno, John E. *The Divided Mind: The Epidemic of Mindbody Disorders.* New York: Harper Perennial, 2007.

Sommer, Adam. "Storytelling with Michael Meade." In *Astrology & the Hermetic Arts: Holes to Heavens,* March 7, 2021. Podcast, website, 68:05. www.holestoheavens.com/storytelling-with-michael-meade/. Retrieved January 2022.

The Myers & Briggs Foundation. "Thinking or Feeling." https://www.myersbriggs.org/my-mbti-personality-type/mbti-basics/thinking-or-feeling.htm. Retrieved January 2022.

Williamson, Marianne. *A Return to Love: Reflections on the Principles of A Course in Miracles.* New York: HarperCollins, 1992.

World Health Organization. "Burn-out an "occupational phenomenon": International Classification of Diseases." *World Health Organization, Departmental news,* May 28, 2019. www.who.int/news/item/28-05-2019-burn-out-an-occupational-phenomenon-international-classification-of-diseases. Retrieved January 2022.

CPSIA information can be obtained
at www.ICGtesting.com
Printed in the USA
BVHW051428030622
638830BV00009B/388

9 781915 229472